GAME

C000154150

Vir Sanghvi is probably the best-known Indian journalist of his generation. He became editor of *Bombay* magazine at twenty-two, making him the youngest editor in the history of Indian journalism. He went on to edit *Imprint* and *Sunday*, then India's largest-selling weekly newsmagazine. From 1999 to 2004, he was Editor of the *Hindustan Times* before being promoted to Editorial Director, a post he held till 2007, after which he continued at the paper as a columnist and advisor. His television career has included several award-winning shows on the Star TV Network, NDTV and CNN-News 18.

He has a parallel career as India's leading food and travel writer. His many books include the best-selling *Men of Steel*, *Rude Food* (which won the Cointreau prize for Best Food Literature book in the world), *Madhavrao Scindia, A Life* and *Mandate: Will of the People*.

By the same author

Mandate: Will of the People

THE
GAME CHANGERS

TRANSFORMING INDIA

VIR SANGHVI

First published by Westland Publications Private Limited in 2019

1st Floor, A Block, East Wing, Plot No. 40, SP Infocity, Dr MGR Salai, Perungudi, Kandanchavadi, Chennai 600096

Westland and the Westland logo are the trademarks of Westland Publications Private Limited, or its affiliates.

Copyright © Vir Sanghvi, 2019

ISBN: 9789388754675

10 9 8 7 6 5 4 3 2 1

Book design by Jojy Philip, New Delhi 110 015
Printed at Thomsona Press (India) Ltd.

MIX
Paper
FSC FSC® C010615

For my mother
who did not live to see me finish this book.
And who I miss every day…

CONTENTS

ACKNOWLEDGEMENTS

Two people powered this book through the years it took to put it together.

The first is my old friend and long-time editor, the long-suffering Sudha Sadhanand whose idea the book was and who never lost her temper with me even when I missed deadline after deadline. Thanks, Sudha. The next one will be on schedule I promise!

The other is my wife, Seema Goswami, who gave up work on her own book to put this one together. She was harsh but thorough, questioning nearly everything I had written and making me work harder than I had ever intended.

Eventually Sudha and Seema cut me out of the editing process, dealt directly with each other and took charge. That's probably why this book finally got published.

Thanks also to Mukesh Rawat, possibly the only person alive who can read my handwriting, for his hard work on the project. And thank you, Tashneem Choudhary for your help with the proofs.

The mistakes, of course, have nothing to do with them and are entirely my own fault.

INTRODUCTION

Over a decade ago, I published a collection of profiles of India's top businessmen (Azim Premji, Ratan Tata, Kumar Mangalam Birla etc.), all based on lengthy interviews. The book did better than I had expected, being translated into several languages and becoming a steady seller over the next few years.

Even now I have people coming up to me and saying how much they learned from the biographical profiles and how so many of the people who featured in the book were their personal heroes. Others have told me how much inspiration they derived from those stories.

Any author is grateful for praise (and for the sales that usually accompany it), so I am always thrilled when people come up to me to talk about the book. (As, oddly enough, they still do, many years after its publication.)

But I am also a little bemused.

Those profiles started out on the business pages of the Mumbai edition of the *Hindustan Times* where I was Editorial Director at the time. We had just launched our Mumbai edition and I wanted the business pages to carry something distinctive. So, once every week (on Tuesday, I think) we would run a full-page profile of some leading business figure. I wrote all of the pieces and spent a large part of each week chasing down top businessmen and getting them to tell me their stories.

I am not modest enough to deny that the profiles were a huge success but they were still, as far as I was concerned, a way of doing a different kind of business coverage to help establish the paper in Mumbai. (We didn't even carry most of the profiles in the Delhi edition where there was enormous pressure on space.)

What I wasn't prepared for was the response we got from people who never normally read the business pages. Would somebody with no interest in business really sit down to read a 2,000-word, full-page profile of some industrialist?

They would. And they did.

Because of the impact the pieces had created, I had the idea of putting them together (suitably updated) in a book. If they had appealed so much to general readers of the *Hindustan Times*, I thought, perhaps they would appeal to people who bought books as well.

It all worked out much better than I had dared hope. What still surprises me when I go to smaller cities is the number of people who can quote incidents from the stories I told in the book. And I am forever astonished by the extent to which people say they found inspiration and encouragement from the guys (and they were all guys) I had profiled in the book.

I still have no clue why the book had this kind of impact. But I do have some tentative observations.

The first is that the more aspirational India becomes, the more we look for inspiring stories. This is—and has been for a decade or so—an India in ferment. In the decades following Independence, we did have ambitions and dreams. But nearly everything we hoped to be was constrained by the circumstances of our birth. If we were born into the families of executives and managers, we hoped to rise up the corporate ladder and get top executive jobs. If we were born into business families we hoped to successfully run the businesses we had inherited. If we studied engineering, we looked for good jobs or tried to immigrate to America.

Sometime in the twenty-first century, the old order broke down. Our dreams ceased to have limits. We began to treat normal existences as futile, as a mark of failure. We wanted, not just to do better than our parents, but to leave them far behind.

The first manifestations of this change came in the way we looked at businessmen. We have always admired successful people, but I doubt if most Indians were as fascinated by rich people as we became in the early years of this century. Kumar Mangalam Birla's father, Aditya was a genius, one of the finest businessmen India has ever produced. (I interviewed him early in my career.) Yet he never possessed anything like the glamour that his son now projects. I was on several flights with him and he hardly got a second glance from the other passengers. Kumar, on the other hand, makes heads turn.

Looking back, I think that was the first phase of our transformation. We had become so admiring of success (and yes, of wealth) that people wanted to read success stories. Rich people became like movie stars, their every action was worthy of interest.

Ratan Tata said to me, in his interview, that he often felt lonely but was too diffident to do anything about it. I thought that this was a remarkably candid admission and I was pleased to have elicited it from him.

But did I think that people would talk about it for years afterwards?

Hardly.

Look at it this way. J.R.D. Tata was one of the few Indian businessmen who can genuinely be regarded as a hero. Quite apart from his daredevilry as a pilot, he managed the nearly impossible feat of running India's largest industrial empire without paying bribes or cutting corners at a time when many of his rivals took a much more—shall we say—'pragmatic' attitude to doing business.

Because JRD continued to run Tatas for so long, he was clearly India's most famous businessman. But if he had told an interviewer that he often felt lonely, would anyone have cared?

Somehow I doubt it.

As the book continued to sell, I realised that I had, entirely unwittingly, struck a lode. There was something going on here that I had not fully understood when I wrote the profiles.

Success was the new romance. Money was the new measure of character. Businessmen were the new heroes.

At that stage at least, there was no pushback against dynasty. Indians took it for granted that business people would come from business families. When they encountered those who went further than their ancestors had ever gone, people were impressed. Azim Premji was born into a wealthy family in the edible oil business. His success in information technology was his own, of course. But nobody minded that his was not a rags-to-riches story. Or that he came from a traditional business background.

So it was with Subhash Chandra, the creator of India's TV boom. He was born into a family of prosperous grain merchants and had never grown up poor. But that, in no way detracted from his success.

The way I saw it, during the first phase of the generational shift in Indian attitudes, people did not need to identify with their heroes. They just needed to admire them and their success.

Sometime over the last five years, the mood changed. I am not sure how it happened or if I can pinpoint the exact moment when India pivoted. But my sense is that the reasons for the shift are both demographic and economic.

The middle class is larger today than ever before. How you measure it is an entirely subjective decision but we know (and something that the late Arun Jaitley, the former Finance Minister, is believed to have once said) that the BJP went into the last general election believing that forty per cent of the Indian electorate is now middle class. Of that forty per cent, something like ninety-five per cent is Hindu (all surveys show that Muslims are near the bottom of the economic ladder). So if a politician has a message that appeals to this constituency, then it is hard to lose a national election.

And what does this constituency want?

It is hard to be specific but if you come from a dynastic background, you have to really excel to get people from this constituency to take you seriously. This is certainly true of the film industry which had become a family business.

Now, if you come from a film background, that is not necessarily a handicap, especially if your success has little to do with your famous parents. (Farhan and Zoya Akhtar are obvious examples; neither benefitted in any way from Javed Akhtar's success as a writer.)

But daddy can't make you a star. I have lost count of the number of male leads who have been launched by powerful filmi parents only to disappear into oblivion over the last three or four years. A famous surname is no longer a guarantee of success or even, of what the industry calls 'initial': the curious people who turn up to see a movie before word gets out about how good or bad it is.

A decade ago, we had come to accept that politics, like films, had become a family affair. The Congress and most regional parties were dependent on dynasty. The Left, which had frowned on family connections was ceasing to matter. Even within the BJP, leaders had begun promoting their sons.

It would be overstating the case to say that the age of dynasty is over (Naveen Patnaik, Jagan Reddy and Stalin, all dynasts, led their parties to electoral success) but it is hard to deny that the old entitlements are more in question in India than ever before.(This is especially so in North India.)

The Congress, for instance, with its front bench full of dynasts, was soundly rejected by the people of India and Rahul Gandhi even lost his own seat. The defeats (including some of the Congress' safest seats) were not predicted by most people who covered the elections. The consensus was that the BJP would form the government but would not necessarily get a parliamentary majority. Hardly anyone saw what was clearly a Modi wave.

In retrospect (and sadly, these analyses always come in retrospect!) what seems clear was that Narendra Modi had captured the imagination of a new middle class. This was at least partly because he presented himself as an outsider, with no sense of entitlement.

What does the new middle class regard as entitlement? The answer has to do with the nature of this emerging middle class. Ever since Manmohan Singh launched the liberalisation programme in 1991, India has been going through more sociological and societal changes than it did in the years from 1947 to 1991.

The first changes were the ones I noticed when my book of business profiles came out. Indians had ceased to think of businessmen as crooked and venal (though some of them clearly were; the corruption of the license raj had allowed many dodgy characters to enrich themselves). They had now begun to admire business people and being rich was considered as a virtue in itself.

But in the decade that followed, much more has changed. Anyone born right after the 1991 reforms is not just an excited teenager as he or she would have been in 2007/8. That generation is now twenty-eight. Others who came of age in the liberalised India (when they were eleven or twelve, say) are now nearly forty. In a country where sixty-five per cent of the population is under thirty-five, this generation constitutes the bulk of the electorate.

It is a generation with hopes and dreams. But it's also a generation with deep resentments. Greater social mobility has meant that much of today's middle class was born into homes where English was hardly spoken and where their parents had 'a sense of place': they believed that they could rise only so far and no further. The best and most glamorous positions in politics, in films, in industry etc., would go to those born into the right families.

This led to resentments among their children and those resentments pretty much define today's middle class. One major focus of the resentment is the English language. Till well into the twenty-first century, social positioning wasn't just about who spoke English (everybody wants to learn English for career advancement) but how they spoke English. Was it grammatically correct? Was it spoken with the right accent, and so on?

Consciously or unconsciously, the traditional middle class let English become the dividing line between old and new. If you spoke English haltingly or if you pronounced the words wrong, then you were always marked as an outsider, as a person who would never quite belong.

In some ways, this is ironic because nearly all Indians, regardless of class, speak English with distinct accents that most native speakers (say, the British) struggle to understand. Yet, even within our accented English, we managed to create sub-divisions, designed not to communicate (which, after all, is the purpose of all language) but to exclude, to remind people of their outsider status.

Till around a decade ago, the divisions of English and accent mattered so much that it was almost impossible to overcome them.

But then social media changed everything. We often don't realise how significant it is that people rarely talk anymore. They send text messages on WhatsApp, they check out Facebook, they post on Instagram or they have little explosions on Twitter. In none of these media does it really matter how well you speak English or what your accent is like.

And social media is a great class leveller. Twitter is still mostly an English language medium (though you can use Indian languages) but the real growth has been in Facebook and WhatsApp in regional languages. A person who speaks bad English and starts out on WhatsApp is on a level playing field with a convent-educated English speaker who is taking to WhatsApp for the first time. Social media has no sense of the complex and insidious divides within the Indian middle class.

So much of what India has become is tied up with the Narendra Modi phenomenon. Convinced after the Gujarat riots that mainstream media would not take Modi seriously, his campaign managers mobilised social media like never before. Shrewdly, they used regional languages to colonise Facebook.

And to this day, Modi's publicists send out 'news' on WhatsApp in various languages. Much of what they send out is, if not downright fake, then certainly tendentious. But for much of the new middle class, which grew up without having the *Times of India*, the *Hindu* or the *Hindustan Times* on their dining tables, this is as real as any other form of news.

Resentment is always a more powerful political tool than actual performance. So people who laid a bet that the BJP would face defeat in the 2019 election because the economy had not done as well as expected failed to understand the mood of the electorate. This was not an election about how the incumbent had performed. It was a rejection of what had gone on before 2014.

So is this a new India?

I don't, for a second, doubt that.

Consider the Cabinet. Of the senior ministers—the prime minister, the Home minister, the Finance minister, the Defence minister and the HRD minister—only the Finance Minister (who has to attend IMF and World Bank conferences) is comfortable in English. Not one (except the Finance minister) went to a well-known school or university. Never before has there been a Cabinet that so decisively rejects English (or what was once so prized: a great university education) with such disdain.

It is not just a class thing. Dr Manmohan Singh, who came from a poorer family than any of today's top ministers, taught himself English and went on to get degrees from Oxford and Cambridge. It is an attitude thing: nobody in this government thinks that any of that is worth the trouble or at all necessary.

Nothing epitomises the current mood as much as the myth-making around Sardar Patel and Pandit Nehru. In popular re-telling, Nehru was an urban sophisticate while Patel looked down on Nehru's secular Western ideas and argued for a more Hindu India. In fact, Patel was a barrister from the Middle

xviii   INTRODUCTION

Temple in London, had a successful law practice in Gujarat, wore Western clothes till he entered politics and, when he was Home Minister, banned the Rashtriya Swayamsevak Sangh or RSS. Most of this is edited out of the myth-making.

The hatred of Nehru is not based on what many might see as his mistakes (his economic decisions were, quite clearly, misguided and wrong) but on his belief in Western liberalism and his notion of a secular India where Muslims were equal citizens with Hindus. His English education, his westernised manner, his alleged affair with a white woman (Lady Mountbatten); these are the issues that are brought up again and again.

Does all of this affect the people who are profiled in this book?

Well, sometimes it does. And sometimes it doesn't.

The book emerged out of a conversation with Sudha Sadhanand who edited *Mandate*, my last book for Westland. Sudha asked if I would do another book of business profiles.

I said that I thought that Indian business had changed so much that there was very little interest any longer in many of the people profiled in the first book. Nor did their stories seem particularly interesting or significant in today's climate.

In fact, I said, of the people I had profiled the first time around, only Nandan Nilekani struck me as being of much interest now because he had managed that most difficult feat of all: he had found a second act in his life. Even if he hadn't been a billionaire in his first stint at Infosys, he was still an important factor in modern Indian life, creating things that would change the way we lived. (Aadhaar, for instance.)

We thought long and hard about the businessmen we would include and settled finally on Vijay Shekhar Sharma who seems to me to epitomise what the new India is all about.

He grew up in a lower middle class family, was not a natural English-speaker and used technology to make his fortune. I believe Paytm and others like it will transform our world.

Vijay's admiration for Modi also made him a natural fit for this book. He is the man who, within hours of the demonetisation announcement on 8 November 2017, had taken front page ads in the newspapers to welcome the scheme and to congratulate the Prime Minister.

How can you include Shashi Tharoor in a book that makes a point of excluding politicians?

Well, because there is much more to Shashi Tharoor than politics. In fact, for the first fifty years of his life, he had no involvement in politics at all.

Though Shashi has done many things in his time (worked for the UN, advised a Dubai-based business conglomerate etc.), only one activity has been consistent through the years: writing.

His first novella was published before he reached his teens and since then he has written consistently and successfully. It is because of his political success that we forget what an accomplished and successful writer he is. Not only are his books bestsellers but they are among the highest selling in the history of Indian publishing.

More significantly, they take a strong ideological stand that is totally at variance with the dominant doctrine in India today. So I included Shashi the writer (not Shashi the politician) to show that in today's India, there is still room for the old liberal-secular consensus if you know how to pitch your ideas.

But nothing is written in stone. When I wrote about Nandan the first time around in *Men of Steel*, I had no idea that he would do so much in the decade that followed to justify a second profile.

So, who knows? A decade from now, there may well be enough to fill a third profile.

As much as India was changing from within, I wanted to capture some sense of how Indians were taking over globally in areas that had traditionally been off-limits to us. When I met Sameer Sain for the interviews for this book, I did not know much about him. (In the two years that have passed, I have got to know him well.) What struck me then was not his success as an investor and entrepreneur, but the level of assurance and confidence he displayed.

He was as much at home ordering Domaine Romanee Conti at the world's finest restaurants as he was eating chaat at Elco in Bandra in Mumbai. Of course he is entirely self-made, but he seemed to me to epitomise a new kind of sophisticated global Indian who could fight it out with the big boys on Wall Street and yet, never compromise even a little on his essential Indianness, no matter who he was dealing with.

Gaggan Anand was a no-brainer. He is the most famous Indian chef in the world (and according to me, the best), winning Michelin stars and topping lists of the greatest chefs and yet, he is still the Punjabi boy from Kolkata, refusing to Frenchify his food or to pretend to be posh or fancy.

I thought Asma Khan made a nice counter-point to Gaggan. (Both are from Kolkata, oddly enough.) She is the only other Indian chef to have featured in the influential Netflix series *Chef's Table* (she is also the first chef with a restaurant in the UK to get on to the show) and remains refreshingly down-to-earth despite her new-found celebrity status. It was a little unsettling though to think that in another life (the 1990s) when I was editor of *Sunday*, she had been a colleague, working as a sub-editor.

The last book had no women, an omission I now regret but which passed largely unnoticed at the time. This time around I was determined to find women who had succeeded in business. Kiran Mazumdar-Shaw was an obvious choice but I was prouder of myself for finding Ameera Shah whose success has passed largely under the radar.

Arnab Goswami was an off-the-wall choice. I interviewed him just as his channel was launched and was roundly berated by other journalists for refusing to be judgemental about his politics. The book is about 'Game Changers' and anyone who denies that Arnab has redefined news television and is the most influential journalist of our times is deluded.

The Arnab chapter was published by Amazon as a stand-alone offering on the net shortly after Republic TV was launched and I have left it as it originally appeared.

I thought long and hard about including Karan Johar mainly because he is already so well-known and there may be little left to say about him. But in almost every way that matters, Karan is a game-changer. Far from being launched by a generous daddy, he actually saved his father's faltering banner. He changed the way movies were made. He chose to become a TV interviewer, transforming forever the celebrity interview show. And though he has refused to come out openly, his obvious lifestyle choices have given hope to lakhs of gay people.

If I was to do this book ten years later or I was to revisit these characters, would they still be around? Would they still be worthy of inclusion?

It is a relevant question because in Modi's India, nothing seems to last forever and everything is constantly changing. One moment Jet Airways is one of the world's best airlines and a month later it has collapsed, its 20,000 employees rendered jobless through no fault of theirs. One moment Anil Ambani is a globally famous billionaire. The next moment he is desperately selling assets in an effort to stay afloat. At one moment, Airtel is the great Indian telcom success story. The next moment, people are wondering if it can hold its own.

So I am wary of making predictions. This is a time of change and great ferment in India. An established elite is being thrown out by a new crowd. All of the old rules are dying or are already dead.

But yes, I will stick my neck out. A decade from now I will still be proud of the choices I made while selecting the people to include in this book.

NANDAN NILEKANI

The last time I wrote about Nandan Nilekani, over a decade ago, he was already a hero-figure for India's educated middle class. Along with a handful of other young professionals, he had followed his boss Narayana Murthy out of a job in Mumbai to set up a small software company in Bengaluru.

Then the global software boom happened and Infosys, the company they founded, took the world by storm. The high quality of its work made it a byword for excellence and its reputation for excellence helped transform the image of India.

Whereas once we had been seen as a low-wages backwater, full of shoddy products and sweatshops, we were now hailed as a knowledge superpower largely on the basis of the high quality, high-tech services provided by Infosys.

Two of Infosys's founders emerged as heroes; the first was Narayana Murthy himself who emerged as the Gandhi of the software generation, with an almost ascetic lifestyle that served as a counterpoint to the excesses of India's other businessmen. Narayana Murthy always travelled economy class, said he cleaned his own toilet and shunned any extravagance.

Murthy's successor as chief executive at Infosys was Nandan, a charismatic and thoughtful person who led the company to even greater prosperity—at one stage Infosys was India's largest company and all its founders were billionaires.

All this made Nandan a celebrity to those who could read without moving their lips. Not only was he rich, he had made his money honestly without ever paying a single bribe. Not only was he a successful CEO, but it seemed like his competence extended beyond software to other things. And not only was he a billionaire, he was also determined to give tens of crores of his money away.

When I did my last long interview with him (which appeared in *Men of Steel*, a collection of profiles of top businessmen) he had found it difficult to move around in Delhi without being recognised. We met at the Taj Mahal Hotel and throughout the interview, people kept staring at him.

He spoke then of his commitment to philanthropy. The reason he had made so much money, he said, was not because he was an extraordinary person but because he was fortunate to be in the right place at the right time. Had he been boss of Infosys when there was no software boom, then the company would not have done as well.

So why was he giving so much of his money away?

The answer was characteristic Nilekani, a mix of the ethicality that is at the centre of his personality and pure common sense. He believed, he said, that people who had made so much by being in the right place at the right time had an obligation to share some of that money with society. Besides, he added, if India's billionaires and millionaires did not let society share in their wealth, this was bound to lead to massive resentment. Consider the great American fortunes, he said, the Rockefellers, the Fords, the Mellons, etc. Every one of these families engaged in philanthropy. This kept a certain balance in American society. We needed to do exactly that in India.

After a spectacularly successful stint as head of Infosys, Nilekani stepped aside because Narayana Murthy believed that all of the founders deserved a crack at the top job. He stayed on at his own company (as Narayana Murthy had) but a new chief executive was appointed.

I wondered then what Nandan would do for a second act. He was too young to retire but somehow, I doubted if he would go back into business. After Infosys, anything else would have seemed like an anti-climax.

His first action was not entirely surprising. He had always been a great thinker, so I was not surprised when he wrote the definitive book on the ideas that had shaped India. It was a huge bestseller all over the world, reaching the *New York Times* bestseller list, and was one of the most successful books ever published in India.

One fallout of the book's global impact was that Nandan became a global celebrity, invited to speak at conferences and universities not in his capacity as a successful businessman, but as a thinker and an author, sharing the stage with academicians and theorists.

But I could not have predicted what would happen next. In 2009, against the odds, the Congress-led UPA was re-elected for a second term. The Congress' leading lights—from Prime Minister Manmohan Singh to Rahul Gandhi—knew Nandan well and soon after the election results were announced, Nandan got a call from Delhi. Could he come and see the prime minister? Would he be interested in being HRD minister?

Nandan had never thought about joining the Cabinet, so he was ambivalent. And in any case, the proposal faced a backlash from Congress leaders who felt that having struggled to win the election, they were entitled to fully partake of the rewards of office. Why should an 'outsider' get one of the top portfolios?

This suited Nandan just fine. He had no interest in becoming HRD minister. Nor was he tempted by jobs like deputy chairman of the Planning Commission. He wanted something that would outlast him and actually make a difference to the way India was run.

One of his ideas was the Unique Identification Number (UID). All of us know that most identity documents in India are vulnerable to fraud. It costs a few hundred rupees to procure a bogus driving license. Voter ID documents are susceptible to fraud. Some people have more than one PAN card.

And yet ID matters. The only way for any welfare scheme to work is if the goods, services and resources meant for the poor actually reach them. And yet in India, welfare schemes are notoriously flawed. Rajiv Gandhi estimated that of every one rupee earmarked for a welfare scheme, only ten paise actually reached the intended beneficiaries. The rest is siphoned off along the way.

What if India could create a scheme whereby the government could accurately identify each person for whom the welfare resources was intended? What if these people could set up bank accounts on the basis of the new identification protocols? The money intended for their welfare could be transferred directly to those accounts so there was little or no scope for leakage or for unscrupulous officials or middlemen to siphon off resources.

Nilekani's formula was simple enough. Assign each person an identity number based not on things like address, which can change, or birth certificates, which most Indians don't have anyway, but on biometrics. Certain physical features—fingerprints, the nature of the eyes, etc., are unique to each of us.

Why not base an identity number on these biometrics? Once the number had been assigned, any Indian could use it to claim his or her share of welfare. Here at last was one way of creating a means of identification that could not be easily compromised.

It sounded simple enough, but the idea of a registry which would contain biometric information was a hot potato. No politician would touch it. And the government was relieved when Nandan agreed to come on board (for a salary of one rupee) to create a unified ID system.

Once he had joined, he realised that almost nobody was on his side. There were those who opposed it openly. Many civil liberties organisations claimed, for instance, that once the government had access to a central registry that contained information about Indians, it could misuse the information.

Nandan countered: How? If the government had biometric information about Indians, why did it follow that it was now in a position to repress the population?

Well, said his critics, suppose an anti-Muslim party came to power. Under this scheme, the regime could identify Muslims.

But couldn't it already do that, Nandan countered. The government had access to voter registration information which included names (from which religion could be inferred) and addresses. How did a few biometric details suddenly make the tyrant's job easier? And so on.

By then, the scheme was called Aadhaar and among its most vocal critics were some members of the government's National Advisory Council (a body that advised UPA chairperson Sonia Gandhi) who echoed the objections of civil libertarians. Eventually Nilekani presented the scheme to Mrs Gandhi and won her support.

Then there was the open opposition of the parties inimical to the Congress. Some of this was based on a political

knee-jerk reaction (if the Congress does it, we must object)
but there were also some genuine doubts and apprehensions.

Nilekani launched a charm offensive. He contacted every
chief minister and significant Opposition leader who had
doubts. He would call on them, he said, and personally explain
why he was so passionate about the scheme. He had Cabinet
rank, so in protocol terms, it was customary for a chief minister
to call on someone of his stature. But Nilekani insisted that he
would visit their state capitals and meet them in their offices.
Or if they were in Delhi, he would call on them in their state
bhawans, homes or offices.

By the end, nearly everyone had come around because
Nilekani was prepared to address every doubt and answer
every question. Even the BJP which had first opposed the
scheme began to see what its merits were. What Nilekani
was not prepared for was the level of concealed opposition.
Much of the civil service worked to sabotage the initiative
because it took away the discretionary power so beloved of
the bureaucracy. To his face the babus (bureaucrats) would tell
him what a wonderful idea it was, while plotting all the while
to strangle the infant scheme in its crib.

It was the same with members of the Cabinet and
politicians who should have been committed to Aadhaar. With
both Manmohan Singh and Sonia Gandhi openly backing the
idea, it was virtually impossible to say that they were against
Aadhaar. But many ministers worked behind the scenes to
scupper the scheme. Sometimes, it was a turf battle: the Home
minister thought Aadhaar was encroaching on his territory.
And sometimes it was personal. Many politicians were jealous
of Nilekani's rapid rise. Some even argued that he could be
the next Manmohan Singh—an honest technocrat put into

government by Sonia Gandhi—and vowed to stop him before it was too late.

If you talk to Nandan about those battles now, he laughs and refuses to name the ministers who were seen as his enemies. But I remember how hassled he seemed at the time, unused to a world where people promised you their undying support and then tried to stab you in the back.

He admits that he coped with some of the opposition by using the skills he had learnt in business. The decision to call on the chief ministers and sell the idea of Aadhaar to them came from his experience of making sales calls at Infosys. There too, he had to call on the heads of powerful companies and persuade them that Infosys was offering a service that they needed.

The bureaucratic sabotage took a little longer to understand. Eventually he worked out that the bureaucracy is like the human body with an immune system that is designed to repel and destroy any outsiders.

The political problems were handled politically. Delhi gossip had it that Nandan had learned how to play the game. Faced with opposition from Chidambaram, the gossips say, Nilekani teamed up with yet another senior leader who apparently had no great affection for Chidambaram but liked Nandan and approved of Aadhaar. Naturally, Nandan laughs off this suggestion and says that he had no problems with P. Chidambaram.

Eventually, he managed to launch Aadhaar and began the massive process of signing people up for it. He succeeded beyond his wildest dreams. Using his managerial expertise, he was able to get a million people to provide their biometric details and become part of Aadhaar in just a few years, a feat that is probably unmatched anywhere in the world.

By the time UPA II's term was coming to an end, Nandan was hailed as one of the most impressive public servants ever and Aadhaar was one of that scandal-hit regime's biggest achievements.

It was time to decide what to do next.

Nilekani says that it wasn't as though the idea of politics had never occurred to him. But pragmatist that he is, he had always put the idea to one side. He did not believe that he was cut out for the rough and tumble of Indian politics and nor was he sure that he could operate within that environment.

But after his success in launching Aadhaar against the odds, he began to reconsider his position. The world of Delhi politics no longer seemed so alien to him and he began to believe that even if he was bound by party discipline, he now had enough understanding of Delhi's political dynamics to make a difference.

And, in many ways, the phrase 'make a difference' summed up what he wanted to do. No matter what you thought of Aadhaar, even its worst critics had to admit that it transformed the way in which governments could identify citizens. But Nandan also realised that there was a limit to how much difference technocrats could make. To achieve much more, he would have to be part of the political system.

The easiest way to do this would be to get elected to the Rajya Sabha. This is the usual means of entry favoured by most technocrats and once you are an MP, you can join the government and become a minister or (as in the case of Dr Manmohan Singh) become Finance minister or even prime minister.

Nandan was reluctant to take this route. He believed that a Rajya Sabha MP still seemed like a technocrat without enough political standing to make a significant difference. He wasn't necessarily right about this. (Manmohan Singh was a Rajya Sabha MP when he dismantled the license-permit-quota raj as Finance minister.) But he believed that if he was going to enter politics, he would plunge head-on into electoral politics.

Towards the end of UPA II's term, Nandan joined the Congress party and announced a little later that he would stand for elections from Bengaluru. His friends told him he was mad. He was standing on a Congress ticket at a time when there was an anti-Congress wave. And while outsiders have been elected to the Lok Sabha before, they have usually made the necessary political compromises. Nandan, on the other hand, would make no compromise. He would say only what he believed. He would only deal in white money and there would be no cash at all in his campaign.

As you probably already know, Nandan lost. It was no big surprise. There was a Modi wave and the Congress was reduced to its lowest ever tally in parliament.

In fact, Nandan seems to have been the only person to be astonished by his defeat. He says that all candidates need to psych themselves into believing that their campaigns are going well and that victory is in sight. Otherwise, they simply can't function.

For a diehard realist like Nilekani, the psyching must have been even more devastating. For once in his life, he let go of reality and of the available evidence (every poll predicted a Modi wave) and worked on building up his morale.

When the inevitable defeat was announced, he took it hard. He had never ever failed at anything he had done in his life. And now he had been defeated in full view of the whole of India which watched the contest with interest.

It took at least three months for scabs to form. And afterwards, he came to certain conclusions about himself. The first was that even though he prided himself on coming from a modest middle-class background and not being some super-Anglicised child of the elite, he realised that his upbringing had been far more privileged than that of most voters. His own reference points, his attitude to religion, his rigid insistence on not going against the spirit of the law: all these made him a misfit in the world of politics.

Or that, at least, is how he sees it. Personally I reckon he is wrong. He was just unlucky to stand against the wave. When he was swept away by the Modi wave, he became convinced of his unsuitability for politics. If he had stood when public sentiment was pro-Congress (five years earlier, for instance) none of the factors he regards as an insurmountable handicap would have seemed that important.

Now that he was out of government, Nandan had to figure out what to do. The Infosys chapter of his life was over, but he was still interested in business. Then there were his other activities. Along with his wife Rohini, he was an active philanthropist, funding causes he believed in. There were also the books. In 2008, *Imagining India* had become a global bestseller, winning favourable reviews. Other books were waiting to be published. And there was the experience in government which he had to put to use.

Eventually, Nandan organised his life by segregating the various things he did. At one level, there were the ideas, captured in the books. (*Rebooting India* came out in 2015.) At another, there was the businessman. He became a serial investor, starting a fund and picking individual start-ups which he believed had promise and required investment from him. Then there was the philanthropy. In 2017, Nandan and Rohini pledged to give away half their wealth, in keeping with the personal philosophy that Nandan had long espoused.

For most people, it would have been enough to be one of India's most prominent public intellectuals, a highly respected investor, a best-selling author and a major philanthropist.

But Nandan wanted more. His great contribution to government had been the idea of using technology to deliver social justice and welfare—one of the original motivations behind Aadhaar. He was convinced that he could still help find solutions to India's governance problems and that all governments could use technology to make administration quicker, easier.

Nilekani had just about finished the process of setting the various aspects of his life into an order that pleased him when an event that few people had predicted occurred.

The original founders of Infosys had walked away from the company. They were all billionaires now and Infosys was flourishing. It seemed like a good idea to go off and try new things (not that any of them ever needed to work again) while they were still relatively young. The company was widely hailed and responsible institutional investors had now come on board. Like the others, Nandan believed that Infosys had outgrown its founders and that the company could only go forward with a new generation of professional managers.

To the outside world, all seemed well with this grand plan till murmurings began in 2017. The founders, it was said, were unhappy with the management, headed by Vishal Sikka, a highly regarded professional. Narayana Murthy was the first to break cover and go public with his misgivings.

He seemed to have two sets of complaints. The first was that the ethical standards on which Infosys had been founded had been breached. The culture of frugality and sense of mission had been abandoned. Huge financial settlements were being offered to executives who left. And so on. A second set of objections was never explicitly stated but was whispered about in corporate circles: the company was not as strong as it appeared to be from the outside and the founders were concerned about Infosys's future. Obviously, they could not say much about this in public because that would damage confidence in Infosys and cause its share price to tank.

The Infosys management defended itself vigorously. The company was doing fine, it said. There had been no breach of ethical standards. There was only one problem, it added, and that was that Narayana Murthy wanted to be consulted on everything. After claiming to have walked away from Infosys, he wanted to feel that he was still in charge of the company he founded.

Murthy said that all the founders were united behind him but his most vocal supporter was Mohandas Pai, an early employee of Infosys who had, in fact, criticised Murthy for denying him the top job on the grounds that only a founder could get it. Now however, Pai, who had gone on from Infosys to become a public figure in his own right, backed Murthy and slammed the management with even greater vigour than Murthy had.

Through all this, Nandan made no public statements. Murthy said that he was in regular touch with Nandan and that the two were on the same page. But when reporters asked Nandan for a comment, he declined. Off the record, he said he was trying to facilitate a conversation between Murthy and the current Infosys management so it would not help for him to go public.

The end had an element of inevitability about it. Either because no management of Infosys could survive if the founders told the public that there was a problem or because there genuinely were issues with Infosys's financial health; the big institutional investors turned against the chairman and managing director of Infosys. Both men had to resign and other directors also quit.

Murthy had won. But nobody knew what came next.

Nandan will not talk about this but the story goes that the heads of various large institutions with investments in Infosys called him and said that the company needed a clean-up. Only somebody who understood Infosys could restore the company to its former glory. He had to come back.

Nandan had no interest in running Infosys again. Nor was he the same person who had once been its brilliant chief executive. Then he had just been one of the founders and the brightest of Narayana Murthy's protégés. Now he was a national figure in his own right, much better known than any of the other founders.

Why would he agree to take a step back and return to Infosys?

But of course, he did it. He overcame his wife Rohini's objections and his own reluctance and agreed to return to Infosys, but only for just long enough to sort the mess and put the company back on track.

He kept his word. In under a year, Infosys was back to being the go-ahead company it had been when he first left and Nandan had found and installed a new chief executive under whom Infosys has continued to deliver excellent results.

So what will Nandan Nilekani do now? He is still in his Sixties, full of energy, with a mind that is bustling with ideas. Retirement is not an option.

So much of what has happened to him has not been his own idea. He would never have worked for the government had he not been invited to. Politics was not his first choice. Going back to Infosys was something he resisted.

It is hard to predict, therefore, what life has in store for him. But here are some of the things I do not believe he will do. He will not try and make more money: it doesn't excite him at all. He won't join politics. He won't become identified with one cause or one political party.

Instead I suspect he will become our first technology-focused public intellectual. There are people with towering intellects in India who participate in public debates on national issues. But very few of them understand technology and the role it has to play in today's world.

My guess is that Nandan will fill the role. As his books demonstrate, he understands the ideas that contributed to the creation of modern India. But unlike most public intellectuals he does not first, have any particular ideological bias. And second, he knows how to translate ideas into action. There is a certain real world pragmatism about him that distinguishes his perspective on India's problems from others.

ASMA KHAN

It is a funny feeling when a colleague from decades ago becomes a success in a totally different field. And it feels even stranger when you find yourself writing a profile of somebody you once knew as a sub-editor.

In 1990, when I edited *Sunday* magazine, a young girl came to ask if she could try her hand at journalism. She worked at Lintas, the ad agency, she said, and wanted to do something different but not entirely unrelated.

I hired her on the spot and all of us in the office thought she was very bright and articulate. Then, a few months later, she announced that she was getting married, resigned her position and went off to live in Cambridge with her new husband.

And that, I thought, was the last I would hear of Asma Khan. Wrong, very wrong.

A few years ago, she sent me an email. She was now a chef in London, she wrote. Not only did she organise private dinners at home but she was also running a pop-up in a pub in Soho. Why didn't I drop in and try her food?

I had to search my memory to remember Asma (time to be candid!) and when I asked old colleagues from the *Sunday* days, they said that they found it hard to believe that she was now a chef.

Then, in 2015, my friend Fay Maschler, London's most influential critic, wrote about Asma's pop-up. It was an unqualified rave review and she rated Asma's little restaurant serving kosha mangsho and kathi rolls ahead of most of London's fancy Indian places.

The day the review came out, there was a line outside the pub where Asma ran her pop-up. It began raining and still the people continued queuing. Asma and her cooks were stunned. But like good Indians, they felt bad for the crowds. So they made little bowls of rice with dal and distributed them for free to those lining up. The gesture did not go unnoticed and every night after that, the small restaurant was packed. It became the cool place to go for people who wanted real Indian food.

'Fay Maschler changed my life,' says Asma now. And indeed, the changes have been dramatic. A year and a half ago, the owners of Kingly Court, a new development off Carnaby Street in the centre of London, offered her a dream deal on a site for a full-fledged restaurant. The restaurant opened to glowing reviews and became a symbol of the new London. Nigella Lawson came. Sadiq Khan, the Mayor of London, praised it. And Asma appeared on the list of the 100 most influential people in food in the UK.

But a few months ago, Asma received her biggest accolade yet. The Netflix series *Chef's Table* has featured some of the world's greatest chefs. It has the power to turn a chef's life around. Gaggan Anand (see p. 104) says that even more than all the honours and awards he has earned (two stars from Michelin, number one restaurant in Asia for an unprecedented four years in a row, etc.), it is *Chef's Table* that made people from all over the world fly to Bangkok to eat at his restaurant.

There has been much heartburn in the UK that no British chef has ever made it to *Chef's Table*.

So when Netflix announced that it had finally selected a British chef, there was much anticipation. To everyone's surprise, they chose Asma.

Before the show aired, I told Asma her life would never be the same again. She would soon be one of the world's most celebrated chefs, the best known Indian chef in the UK and perhaps globally, with the exception of Gaggan.

As wonderful as all this is, a little voice inside my head kept asking, How did Asma, the same old Asma from the *Sunday* desk, end up becoming one of the great chefs to be featured on *Chef's Table*? Had she been a secret cook all along even as she laboured over copy? Had she worked at some of the world's best restaurants? Had she reinvented classic Indian dishes?

The answer: none of the above.

The Asma story is so incredible that if you made a movie with this plot, you would be accused of asking too much of the viewer. Suspension of disbelief is okay, but Asma's life takes us far beyond that.

Asma was born in Kolkata but her family's roots were from all over India. Her father's family came from Uttar Pradesh and her mother's people had settled in Jalpaiguri in eastern India. They spoke Hindi at home and because they lived in Kolkata and her mother had a Bengali-speaking background, Asma was also fluent in Bengali.

Her parents both came from land-owning families—what we would call (if we were being nice) nawabi backgrounds or (if we were not so nice) zamindari heritage. While there were vast landholdings and country houses in UP, the family was never cash-rich. Like all old families of their background, they had more than enough money to maintain a comfortable upper middle-class lifestyle but they were by no means rich. Asma never thought of herself as a Bengali, a north Indian or even as a Muslim. 'I was brought up as a child of undivided India,' she says. Though she was born long after Partition, I know what she means. There have always been families who reject the forced separation that politics has imposed on the sub-continent and enjoy the magnificent culture and heritage of pre-Partition India.

For all that, she had the standard well-bred young lady's education. She went to school at La Martiniere, Kolkata, and then to college at Loreto. By the time she graduated, she was done with academics and ready to work. She found a job at Lintas, the advertising agency, and then left after a few months to join *Sunday*.

She says she was quite content to continue working in journalism when her parents introduced her to Mushtaq. 'I guess it was a set-up, in retrospect,' she says. 'But at the time I met him, I really liked him.' Mushtaq was a brilliant Bangladeshi economist who was a don at Sidney Sussex College in Cambridge.

Mushtaq liked Asma too and in no time at all they were married. Asma gave up her job at *Sunday* and moved to Cambridge to be with her husband. Almost without realising it, she had become part of the classic South Asian experience: an educated girl in an arranged marriage who had left her friends and family behind and moved to a foreign country.

She was miserable. 'I thought the Quran had it wrong when it described hell,' she recalls. 'Hell was Cambridge.' She hated the cold, the greyness, the drab English environment (especially after the sights, smells and sounds of Kolkata).

Though her mother had run a catering business in Kolkata, Asma did not know how to cook. She could read copy, she could give clever headlines. But she had no kitchen experience. Fortunately Mushtaq had no interest in food.

So she turned to academics. She chose Law and worked towards a degree. 'It started out as a way of passing the time and keeping myself occupied. Mushtaq was always working and I thought that I needed to do something that I could do by myself to shut out the cold greyness of England.'

By the time she got her Law degree, Mushtaq had been offered a senior position at the School of Oriental and Asian Studies (SOAS) in London and the family moved. She had the option of trying to find something else to do in London but she decided to stick with academics.

She went and saw the Law department at King's College, London, and asked if she could study for a doctorate. The college pointed out that she didn't even have a master's degree yet but Asma, who is nothing if not persuasive, convinced the tutors that she was ready for a shot.

She chose an interesting if slightly academic subject for her thesis: the difference in the way the law treats religion in the UK and the US. 'It interested me a lot,' she recalls. 'In the UK, whatever the actual day-to-day practice, there is no legal framework for a separation of Church and State. The monarch is head of the government and also head of the Church of England. In the US, on the other hand, there is a constitutional basis for the separation of Church and State and all the laws have to pass a test to see that they do not, in any way, mix religion with politics.'

By the time her thesis was nearing its end, Asma was restless again. Mushtaq was travelling a lot and each time she was alone at home, she longed to find something new to do.

Then, some long forgotten cooking gene deep inside her reasserted itself. There is a cooking tradition in her family. Her mother ran a catering business. Her family has always been proud of its recipes, some of which have been regarded as closely guarded secrets. One of her ancestors grew the mango that would later go on to become Pakistan's favourite fruit.

But Asma had always turned her back on this tradition. In part, it was the old Indian cliché. As a woman, you either became the mother who cooked for the family or the woman who went out and worked. Because of her obvious intelligence, Asma had always chosen to work or study. But now she began to wonder why she could not do it all.

She asked her mother for recipes and began experimenting in her kitchen. The results were so satisfying that she considered setting up her own catering business. She found South Asian women in London who were great cooks but had few opportunities to cook for anyone outside their families.

Apart from the newly discovered cooking skills, Asma had one other advantage. 'Mushtaq's family had an up and down relationship with money,' she explains. 'Sometimes they were up and sometimes they were really down. By the time we shifted to London, they had lost pretty much all of their glamorous properties. But they did have one remaining asset to give us: a house on Old Brompton Road (an upmarket part of London). It was a lovely old house but it was too big for us. There were winters when Mushtaq and I could only afford to heat one room so we would do everything—eating, sleeping, everything!—in that room.'

Now Asma decided to put the house to good use. She began organising small pop-up dinners at her home. She asked the South Asian women she had discovered in London to help her in the kitchen and in no time at all, well-heeled Londoners were raving about her food.

There was a problem, of course. Mushtaq had no idea that his wife was hosting these dinners. She scheduled them during his frequent absences and never told him what she was up to. 'We used to clean the house so well after the dinners that when he came back to London, he had no idea what had gone on!' she laughs.

But her two children, who were not happy with having the house taken over by strangers, complained to their father and soon the jig was up.

Asma is nothing if not super-confident, so she called such famous London chefs as Cyrus Todiwala and Vivek Singh to her house for dinner to try her biryani. Even though none of them knew her, they came anyway. They were kind and encouraging. Vivek Singh was so impressed that he offered her a pop-up at his Cinnamon Club restaurant. She took her all-woman team of cooks and won over the all-male Cinnamon Club kitchen team. ('I will always be grateful to Vivek for that,' she says.)

It was her time in the Cinnamon Club kitchen that convinced her that she and her all-woman team of chefs could run a restaurant. 'I saw how the chefs were initially so dismissive. And my team was also diffident and tentative. But the kitchen is a great leveller. When the Cinnamon Club chefs tasted the food my cooks had made, they realised that it was good. After that,' she recalls, 'there was not only mutual respect between both sides but they also began to get along and enjoyed coming together.'

That gave her the credibility to do a fulltime pop-up. Word of her skills got out. Fay discovered her. And the rest is the stuff *Chef's Table* episodes are made of.

I asked Asma why she called her restaurant Darjeeling Express. Partly, it turns out, there was an element of nostalgia to the name. Because her mother came from Jalpaiguri, she often took the train to Darjeeling and she still remembered the food smells that hit her nose when the train crossed into the populated areas. But there was a practical reason as well. She wanted a name that was non-cuisine specific.

One easy way out would have been to choose a name that reflected her Kolkata upbringing or even something that referenced Bengali food. After all, Asma grew up in Bengal and her husband is a Bangladeshi.

But she took a deliberate decision to avoid any overt Bengali references. There is Bengali food on the menu but Darjeeling Express is not a Bengali restaurant. Because she sees herself as a child of undivided India, Asma wants to retain the option to serve food from anywhere—from north India (she has many ancestral UP recipes), from Bangladesh, from west Punjab or even from south India.

It is not an alien concept to us in India where the same roadside restaurant may serve both channa-bhatura and dosas (or even Manchurian—but that's another story!) because as Indians have travelled around the country, cuisines have cross-pollinated. But it is relatively unusual in London where Indian restaurants are dominated by the regional origins of the cook or are posh and 'modern'.

Now, with the success of Darjeeling Express, Asma is well-known in London. People make much of her nearly all-woman team. (My wife, who came to lunch at Darjeeling Express with me, loved the female energy; she was sold on the restaurant even before the first dish arrived.) Asma is overtly political, speaking out about sexual harassment in restaurant kitchens, breaking the conspiracy of silence that women in the business have gone along with, and has become a symbol of the success that Asian women can find if they overcome prejudice and their own apprehensions.

But ultimately, I judge chefs by their food, not by their stories. And Asma's was terrific. We had puchkas, Bihari phulkis (like pakodas), kosha mangsho, a Kolkata mutton chap, kaala chana, chicken samosas, beetroot chops and so much more. None of it was molecular or clever-clever. It was just excellent.

You will hear more about Asma in the months ahead. After Gaggan, she is Kolkata's second contribution to the global food world.

But I suspect you will also hear about Asma in non-food contexts. When you talk to her, it is clear that she loves food. But it is just as clear that food is only one of her interests. She is one of the most politically aware chefs I have met and has strong views on nearly everything. She wants to fight for women's issues but she also worries about turning herself into a cliché.

Certainly, it would be easy to see her as an example of a modern British Asian Muslim woman who is stepping out and creating careers for herself and her cooks. Except that Asma's life does not fit into any British-Asian or Muslim woman cliché. She did not even grow up in the UK; she had already been a journalist by the time she arrived in Britain. Her experiences are not those of the women from Brick Lane; the first place she worked at or studied in was Oxbridge. She did not start cooking in the East End but in a very nice house on the Old Brompton Road. She had a bright and supportive husband—eventually, when she wanted to open Darjeeling Express, Mushtaq put his life's savings in the restaurant.

But equally, because she understands the cultural background, she can relate to young South Asian women who come to the UK after arranged marriages. And now, because she has the power to do something, she wants to help them.

Nor are her ambitions restricted to the UK. She is working on a project to open an all-woman kitchen in Syria, the first in a series of kitchens that she wants to open in conflict zones.

Sometimes I wonder if this sort of project matters to her more than the food does. And perhaps it does. As she says: 'I don't want to be remembered as a great chef. I want women to come to my grave and say, "She changed my life". That's what really matters.'

She is not short on confidence and ambition, our Asma. And I have a feeling that she will end up being the most successful person to ever emerge from the offices of *Sunday* magazine!

KARAN JOHAR

There are many reasons why Karan Johar should be in this book, the most important being that he helped create a new genre of Hindi cinema that pretty much changed the rules of the game. And that he invented a new kind of celebrity talk show and made it impossible for any TV presenter who was less well-connected than him (i.e., every single TV presenter) to do a show that was as entertaining or informal.

But I didn't choose him for either of those reasons. I chose him because he is the renaissance man of Indian cinema, a top director who wants to be so much more: talent show judge, actor, dancer, master of ceremonies, producer, author and god alone knows what else.

And because, in a country (and an industry) where nobody likes being honest about sex or sexuality, he has the guts to be himself.

First things first: is Karan Johar gay?

Yes. He probably is. He does not deny it and his conversations seem to assume that the person he is talking to knows that he is gay.

But here's the thing: he won't come out and say it. Not because he is ashamed of his sexuality but because he believes that there should be no obligation for gay people to come out.

Sexuality is a private matter and it is nobody else's business. People can reveal as much about their sexuality as they choose—but only because they want to, not because somebody expects them to.

Which is fair enough. Except that sexuality seems to have played a major role in Karan's life. Even as a child he recalls being treated as a fat boy with effeminate gestures. He was, he concedes, probably very effeminate but was unprepared for the scorn that was heaped on him or the names that he was called: 'pansy' was the most common.

The jeering made him uncomfortable with his sexuality and for years he struggled with his own preferences. He went on diets and lost weight. He thought that perhaps his style of talking drew the wrong kind of attention to him so he went to classes to learn how to modulate his voice. He worried about his walk so he went to another instructor to learn how to walk.

But these were external manifestations of his personality. Inside, he was still the same. He tried to pretend that he was like the other boys. When they said they had crushes on girls, he tried everything possible to fit in.

Even success did not help settle the conflicts that raged inside him. When his first movie *Kuch Kuch Hota Hai* released in 1998, when Karan was twenty-six, the director was still a virgin. The movie went on to become a super-hit and launched a new genre in which the characters came from different backgrounds, wore designer clothes, had an international outlook on life, and focused on romance to the exclusion of nearly everything else.

Even as the film smashed box-office records and established Shah Rukh Khan as the king of romance, its director remained a shy, under-confident virgin who had never known any kind of romance in his own life.

He had, he says, a bad case of unrequited love in his Twenties and the rejection was so great that it was 'worse than having a tumour in the brain.' It caused anxiety, breathlessness, and gave him a sense of emotional emptiness.

He had success and money now. But it made no difference to his inner confidence. Sex had always been something of a mystery to him. ('I was very backward in this department,' he says) and it took him a long time to even understand the mechanics. Till he was out of school, he did not know what the words 'fuck' and 'masturbation' meant.

And when he thought he did know what those terms meant, he was usually wrong. Take the term 'blow job'. He had no idea what it meant till a classmate told him, 'You take off all your clothes and put your fan on high speed and that's a blow job.'

Karan was so curious about the mystery of sex that he went home and did just that.

It felt good and later, he bragged about his blow jobs, 'I had three blow jobs yesterday,' he announced proudly.

By the time he was twenty-six and one of India's hottest young directors, he had figured out that fans were not required for blow jobs. But he had still never touched another person sexually. He longed for physical intimacy and to be touched.

After the super success of *Kuch Kuch Hota Hai*, he declared that he needed to do something about his virginity. He had heard about a high-end escort service in London and decided he would pay for sex just to find out what it was like.

But even that decision was accompanied by a lot of trauma. He felt he was overweight. What would it be like taking off his clothes in front of a stranger? Would the other person laugh when he saw Karan's naked body? Then he rationalised. He was paying for the sex. How did it matter what the other person thought?

So he decided to go ahead. He met the escort, paid the money and then, just as proceedings were about to commence, decided that he couldn't go through with it. He told the escort to keep the money and ran away.

A week later he decided to try again. This time he did muster up the courage to have sex and finally managed to lose his virginity.

It was, he recalls, fun at a physical level. And the release was something he needed badly. But after it was through, he still felt empty. Because the escort had only been doing a job, the whole experience felt fake. 'It felt like I was in a film with cameras on.'

He hasn't paid for sex since (though he was tempted to do so once in New York, a decade or so ago) and has come to terms with his sexuality though he doesn't seem to have found the kind of fulfilling romance that features in his movies. He has been in love, he says. And he has had sex. But the two have not gone together. He has not had sex with anyone he loves.

As painful as this personal journey has been, it has not been helped by the mocking, sneering attitude of people. In some ways, it is as though the boys who once called him a fairy have now grown up and still hang around saying the same sort of thing. And now that he is famous, more people recognise him and comment on his sexuality.

Sometimes, it is strangers. He has been at airports, he says, when so-called fans have walked up to him and asked, 'So Karan, are you a homo?' Another time, at another airport, he was minding his own business in the lounge when a family walked up to him, told him how much they admired him, and asked if they could be photographed with him. Because he is the kind of guy who believes in being nice to his fans in all circumstances, Karan was happy to oblige.

Then one member of the family spoke up. 'Thank you so much, Karan,' he said. 'You know my wife doesn't really like homosexuals, but even then, we like you.'

As he says now, 'There was just so much that was objectionable in that statement that it took my breath away!'

Interviewers are as inquisitive about his private life. He was giving an interview about a business venture one morning when the anchor suddenly asked if he was a homosexual. Another time, the interviewer asked straight out if it was true that he was having an affair with Shah Rukh Khan.

This time, something snapped inside Karan. He asked the TV anchor, 'Are you having an affair with your brother?' The anchor was horrified. 'Of course not,' he responded. 'Why are you asking me that?'

'Well,' said Karan, 'because that is exactly the sort of question you have just asked me. Shah Rukh is like a member of my family and yet you think I am having an affair with him.'

Sometimes the questions can come when least expected. A decade ago, I was anchoring a session at the Hindustan Times Leadership Summit with Karan and Saurav Ganguly. We turned to the audience for questions. Most were thoughtful and sensible—about how it felt to be big achievers at such young ages etc. Then a very senior civil servant at the back of the hall put up his hand. I called on him to ask a question, sure that a man of his eminence would have something substantial to ask.

Not much luck.

'Tell me, Karan,' began the civil servant. 'What about all these stories about you and Shah Rukh Khan? Are they true?'

I was taken aback. And so I imagine was Karan who tried to frame an appropriate response, given that he was at a high-powered summit and that the question had been asked by an eminent person.

Finally, he fell back on saying that the question was unfair to Shah Rukh who was clearly heterosexual, was happily married, and had two children (he now has three). 'As Shah Rukh himself has pointed out,' Karan responded, 'you don't create children with heavy petting. You need to go a little further...'

The audience laughed but the question had clearly (and justifiably) irked Karan. And the stories about Shah Rukh and him refused to go away. Finally, both men got tired of issuing denials and decided to make a joke of it.

Some of the stories, Karan remembers, were so ridiculous that he was astonished people even took them seriously. 'One rumour was that somebody had chanced upon Shah Rukh and me in the Concorde Lounge at London airport and we were breathlessly making out,' Karan recalls. 'That was just so absurd. Even if we were having a clandestine affair, would we be kissing in a public place like an airport lounge?'

Eventually, Shah Rukh jokily alluded to the rumours when he appeared on Karan's TV show. Karan asked him, 'What if you wake up as Karan Johar?'

Shah Rukh shot back, 'My chances of waking up as him are less. But waking up with him are more.'

But in a country where many people have still to learn what irony means, some gossips took this as confirmation of the rumours.

For years even as Karan battled speculation about his private life, he refused to discuss his sexuality. Then, in 2017, he published his memoirs titled *An Unsuitable Boy*, in which many of the stories about his early sexual confusion were revealed. When I read it, I was surprised to find that virtually every story one had heard (plus many that nobody had heard before), from the late loss of virginity to an escort, to his confusion about what a blow job is faithfully recounted.

Too much information?

Why did one of Hindi cinema's top directors and a nationally recognised celebrity want to tell us that he had never managed to have sex with anyone he loved?

Soon after the book was published and shocked readers with its honesty about sexual matters, I sat down with Karan for a TV interview. Why was there so much sex in the book? I asked. Did he really mean it when he said that he still did not have enough sex?

Yes, he said, he did. That side of his life had never quite sorted itself out. And he felt it was important to talk about sex for several reasons. One: there was no point writing a memoir if he wasn't going to be entirely honest. Two: there had been so much speculation about his sex life that it was time to finally put the truth on record.

But there was a third reason, and this was the most important. He can't have been the only boy who was called 'fatty' or 'pussy' at school. There must be other kids out there who face the same kind of humiliation and ridicule. It was important to let them know that they were not alone. Others had been in that same situation before and managed to successfully overcome that phase of their lives.

As for the candour about his sexual identity and the confusion he felt about growing up when he was not attracted to girls? Well, surely there are still thousands of boys out there who are as confused. In a country where the 'love that dare not speak its name' is not a cliché but a brutal reality, it is important for people in the public eye to be honest about their own sexual confusion and struggles.

Wasn't he worried that the sexual candour in the memoir would detract from his many other achievements, some of which were not even mentioned in the book?

No, he wasn't. He wanted the book to capture who he was. And he was essentially a product of those insecurities and confusions. Why lie about that?

It's been close to two years since the book appeared and I think Karan has been proven right. The sniggering about the sexual anecdotes has died down (as have the Shah Rukh Khan rumours) and most people now accept that yes, Karan is gay but it hardly matters. In that sense, he has helped people with different or complicated sexualities find greater acceptance and has contributed to the normalisation of the public perception of homosexuality.

His achievements are too massive and too memorable to ever be overlooked. Yet, he feels, with some justification, that a professional caricature of his life is still firmly imprinted in the public mind.

According to this caricature, he is the spoilt rich son of film industry parents who makes movies about rich people and perpetuates the filmi tradition of dynasty. In his memoir, he recalls a conversation with the director Zoya Akhtar who once told him delightedly that people were calling her the new Karan Johar.

He says he told her, 'Don't take it as a compliment. They don't mean it as a compliment. They mean you are making a film about rich people and frivolous things that don't matter.'

And that, in fact, is the one raw nerve when it comes to his work. He is annoyed by the way in which the work is pigeon-holed. 'I am told that I make NRI films,' he says. 'What is an NRI film? I am told I make films about families. Only one of my films has been about a family. I am told I make romances. Only one of my films has been romance.'

He reckons that people often confuse the persona with the movies. He never gets credit for *My Name is Khan*, for instance, which dealt with the perception of Muslim identity. Or *Kabhi Alvida Naa Kehna* which was about infidelity. (He remembers: 'I had people writing mails to me saying, "From loving your parents to leaving your wife, what kind of departure is this?"')

He says, with just the slightest trace of bitterness, 'I think if my name was not Karan Johar, but Karan Kaushik or something like that, then people would praise me for taking chances or for making edgy films.'

The bitterness is justified. He is a child of the industry only in the loosest sense. I knew his father, Yash Johar, a little. He was regarded as the nicest man in the industry, ready to help anyone at a moment's notice. Yash had his own business and lived in Malabar Hill, far away from the studios of Bollywood. So Karan's childhood was hardly a typical filmi affair. His parents did not socialise with film stars and Karan did not grow up with film kids. They were comfortably off in an upper middle class, Malabar Hill sort of way, but they were never rich. As nice a man as Yash was, he was not lucky as a producer. Film after film would flop and he would end up with losses. Often the films were good but failed at the box-office. For instance, *Agneepath*, one of his last films, showcased one of Amitabh Bachchan's best performances but lost money. Then Johar had to sell a property they owned to make up the losses.

So Yash Johar was not a millionaire producer who decided to launch his son as a director. Karan wrote his first script (*Kuch Kuch Hota Hai*) under the mentorship of Aditya Chopra and the film only became viable when Shah Rukh Khan (who Karan had met on the sets of *Dilwale Dulhania Le Jayenge*) agreed to star in it. At the time, Yash could not believe that a big star like Shah Rukh would agree to star in a movie made by his inexperienced son. When *Kuch Kuch Hota Hai* became a super hit, it made more money than all the films that Dharma (the family banner) had produced, put together.

So Karan's background is complicated because he is of the industry and yet, is an outsider. My own sense is that it is this unusual (at least in Karan's generation) mixture of Malabar Hill westernisation and Bollywood glamour that gave Karan his own special niche.

As he recalls, when he was growing up, his friends and their parents would never watch Hindi movies and would even look down on them. In some snobbish way, they regarded Hindi films as being for the masses while they themselves would watch only English movies. Because Karan came from what could be regarded as a South Bombay-English movies sensibility, he made films that would appeal to people like him. Fortunately, the release of the early films (*Kuch Kuch Hota Hai, Kabhi Khushi Kabhie Gham*, etc.) coincided with a demographic and attitudinal change in India.

Seven years after the economy had been opened up and liberalised, Hindi cinema had yet to recognise that there was a young, new audience out there who liked the idea of a heroine in a DKNY top and designer trainers. Karan was the first to get this audience, more by instinct than design, I suspect—and found huge success as a consequence.

The positive aspect of all this is that there are no longer Hindi movie people and English movie people. Even affluent westernised urban Indians love Hindi movies.

Film stars were once regarded as being slightly vulgar. Now they are the toast of Mumbai society. The old barriers have completely collapsed.

The negative side, from Karan's perspective, is that because he changed the trajectory of Hindi cinema, he will forever be associated with films about rich people in designer clothes who spend lots of time in America and Europe. It doesn't matter that Karan has extended himself far beyond the scope of his first two or three movies that are more urban and upmarket than the other Hindi films of the time as a consequence of the change in filmmaking he pioneered. Once you are an agent of change, you are forever identified with that change.

Karan joked to me about how people see him as a 'Bollywood Mogul' who runs everything along with his rich pals. (The actress Kangana Ranaut has turned Karan-bashing into a nice little cottage industry.) He was right to scoff at the caricature but at the same time, it is true that Dharma is now a Bollywood powerhouse, discovering and launching talent and hiring other directors to make its movies.

Strangely, this success doesn't seem to be enough for Karan. Even as the Dharma machine launches away, he is off doing new things. The Koffee With Karan TV show, the most successful English language series in the history of Indian TV, keeps coming back season after season.

But Karan also does many other things that he has no real reason to do: anchoring award functions, dancing at public functions, acting in movies, being a judge on talent shows, etc. It can't be the money that makes him do it. So I guess he just likes extending himself, going from adventure to adventure.

He was forty-five when his memoir came out. And in that book, one legacy of the first half of his life is clearly spelt out. 'I have brought homosexuality to dining table discussions. I have received over a thousand emails and letters from gay boys.... I always feel that the biggest homophobic men and women in this country are definitely oppressed homosexuals.'

So yes, he has forced Indians (gently and with humour) to confront our troubled sexualities. That is a major achievement. And I believe that he gets the credit for it.

But his second achievement—changing the sensibility of Hindi cinema—either goes unrecognised or is discussed with sneers like 'Karan Johar-type films about rich people?' That is an injustice. And I hope that one day he gets the credit for that.

But as he said when I last interviewed him, the memoir is a tale of only half a life. He has many decades to go.

And who knows what he will come up with in the years to come.

AMEERA SHAH

What is it that turns somebody from a non-business family into an entrepreneur, I asked Ameera Shah, the managing director of Metropolis Healthcare (a multinational chain of diagnostic labs with one hundred and fifty labs and fifteen hundred collection centres over seven countries). What made her decide to go into business?

I don't know if she had the answer. But she did have some insights.

Shah's parents are doctors in Mumbai. Her mother is a successful gynaecologist with a practice at Kemp's Corner and her father, a pathologist, ran a lab in Gamdevi called Dr Sushil Shah Lab. She has one sister who is a geneticist in the US. But Ameera herself never had any interest in medicine or science.

She is not even sure she had much interest in studies. 'I don't know if I would use the term "tomboy,"' she says. 'But I was always more interested in outdoorsy pursuits and sport than I was in studies. I did okay in school but I never got top grades or anything.'

Instead, she credits trekking with helping her succeed in business. 'When you are trekking you are at the mercy of nature,' she explains. 'You could hit a storm, it could rain, so many different things could happen. You quickly come to terms with the idea that you are in an environment that you have no control over. Anything can happen and you have to learn to manage.'

Business, she suggests, is a little like that. You set out on an adventure but you never quite know what the atmosphere will be like on the journey and whether there will be any storms along the way. But if you have learned your lesson from trekking, then you know that you just have to cope and keep going or at least, find a way forward.

I confess that I had never thought of it that way. These days we think of people in business as having learnt their lessons at management schools and not in the great outdoors. But for Shah, it was her love of trekking and of venturing out of her safe, Cumballa Hill comfort zone (she lived on Warden Road and went to Greenlawns High School nearby) that gave her the confidence to go into business.

Even then, she says, the early steps were more opportunistic and not part of any great master plan. She went to the University of Texas (after a stint at Mumbai's HR College) at Austin over an Ivy League school ('I am not sure my grades were good enough for the top colleges, anyway,' she says frankly).

As part of her course, she got the opportunity to intern at Goldman Sachs, the Holy Grail for aspiring Masters of the Universe. But the experience left her cold. She did not like the atmosphere or the energy and was unimpressed by the emphasis on big money and high finances.

She also worked briefly at a start-up in Texas and she thought that was much more fun. Looking back, she thinks that perhaps those two experiences provided an indication of what was to follow. She has not been a big institution-power player kind of person. She has enjoyed business much more when it seemed like an adventure.

When she returned to Mumbai, she looked at her father's lab and wondered if there was a future in joining the business. Her father was something of an oddity in the field. In those days, the lab did not do the standard tests because hospitals and clinics were happy to do those themselves. But more complicated tests were referred to Dr Shah's lab because he had a reputation for excellence as a pathologist. But even though he was entirely dependent on the trade for his business (only a tiny proportion of the tests were conducted at the behest of individual consumers or patients), he refused to pay kickbacks to those who could send business his way. (In those days, it was routine for specialists and labs to pay off those who referred patients or sent samples for testing; perhaps it still is, for all I know.)

Dr Shah had thought of expanding but he wanted to do it on the basis of friendship and relied on recommendations from friends. He heard of an opportunity in Chennai and partnered with a lab there. He asked a friend who was in the medical equipments business to come on board as a partner. And when he changed the name of the lab to facilitate the expansion, he chose Metropolis which was suggested by his wife.

When Ameera joined the business, the environment at work was not ideal for a young person who wanted to leave a mark on the company. First of all, her father's partner had an equal share of the business and he did not take her particularly seriously. Secondly, even her father's key employees, who were used to a certain way of doing things, regarded her as a young girl with no medical background who had only turned up at the office because her father's name was on the door. And thirdly, the company had no professional management and no growth strategy. 'When we did expand by buying over another lab,' she recalls, 'all the expansions were ad-hoc. Somebody came to us with an offer and we liked it, so we bought the lab. There was no plan in place at all. Many of those opportunistic expansions proved to be big mistakes and later we had to extricate ourselves from them.'

Shah realised quickly that if any expansion plan was to succeed, the company would have to understand that it was not just a lab conducting tests but an organisation that offered medical service to customers. That change in the basic DNA of the company was not easy to bring about, nor was it easy for her to put in place financial systems, an HR department, marketing policies and the other essentials of a modern organisation.

Through it all, she was determined to make Metropolis grow. The company acquired labs in Kerala, tied up with a Sri Lankan hospital, and then began expansion in the Middle East. Africa came next and the company explored opportunities in Britain.

In the midst of all this, Ameera met a UK-based NRI while discussing a possible tie-up, married him and finally moved out of her parents' home to nearby Peddar Road. The marriage was not a success. Though she is careful not to blame her husband for its failure ('There are always two sides when a marriage goes wrong'), it was no secret that there was considerable turbulence in her home.

I asked her how she coped with all the tensions. She had managed to put her imprint on Metropolis, but her relationship with the business partner had not improved. So she faced a tense situation at work and came home every day to more tension.

How did she keep going? Didn't the constant stress ever get her down? After all, she had no training for running a successful company that was expanding at such a furious rate.

She was learning each day on the job. And yet, everywhere she looked, she found only tension and conflict.

Shah falls back again on the trekking metaphor to explain her state of mind during this phase. Yes, there were storms, she says, but she knew she just had to find a new route to keep going.

But weren't there days of depression? Of feeling like giving up?

Yes, there were, she admits. But she kept going anyway. In 2006, Ameera decided that if the company was really going to expand, it could not do so on the basis of internal accounts. Metropolis went to ICICI Ventures and sold a stake. From that stage on, the company became less a partnership between two squabbling entities and more a professionally-run corporation. In 2010, ICICI Ventures sold its stake to Warburg Pincus, the company continued to grow all over the world, and profits rose.

At some stage, however, tensions have a way of needing to be resolved. Shah ended her marriage and moved into a new flat (down the road again, on Altamount Road), so her personal life took on a semblance of normalcy. But the tensions with the partner remained till Warburg decided it wanted to exit.

Ameera decided that she had to end the stalemate. She borrowed 550 crores from KKR India, the local branch of KKR, the US private equity firm, and bought Warburg's stake.

This gave her a sixty-three per cent stake in the company versus her erstwhile partner's thirty-six per cent. So she finally had total control. But it came with a heavy price: a debt of 550 crores at a massive interest rate of around eighteen per cent.

I asked Ameera how she coped with the stress of the battles. She says that it was so bad that even though she usually manages to sleep soundly in most circumstances, she found that her sleep patterns were ruined. She would wake up at 3 a.m., her fists clenched, and worry about how the situation would be resolved.

And even the resolution has not really felt like victory because she has a huge debt. 'I come from a professional middle-class background,' she explained. 'So I am never comfortable with the idea of debt. And never ever did I imagine that my debt would reach such stratospheric levels.'

On the other hand, even if you factor in the debt, Ameera is now rich. Very rich. Current estimates of the value of her shares in Metropolis vary, but the company is worth 5,000 crores, so her sixty-three per cent stake is worth over 3,000 crores, which puts the debt of 550 crores in perspective. Moreover Metropolis is growing and though she is evasive about discussing it, there is a high probability that the company will go public in the near future, making her a billionaire.

When you consider that she has just turned forty (she was born in 1979) and started out with nothing more than her father's pathology lab in Gamdevi, this is a considerable achievement.

But I am not sure she gets the credit she deserves. Some of this has to do with the structure of Indian business where nearly everyone you will read about is the son or daughter of a very rich businessman. Because Metropolis grew out of Dr Sushil Shah's Lab, many people think she is merely the new generation of an established business family. After all, wasn't it her father who founded the business?

Her father makes no such claims for himself and freely acknowledges that Metropolis would not be the 5,000 crores company it is today without Ameera's entrepreneurial skills. But still, the articles will talk about the 'Shah group-run Metropolis, or Ameera Shah, daughter of the founder of Metropolis.'

Some of it also has to do with the fact that she is a woman. Indians have got used to the success of women abroad (Indra Nooyi is the shining example) and recognise that many of our leading bankers are women (Shikha Sharma, Arundhati Bhattacharya, Naina Lal Kidwai, etc.). But when it comes to woman entrepreneurs in businesses that are usually run by men, the tendency is to assume that when women are in charge, they are wives or daughters.

In some ways, Ameera has had the best of all worlds. She has expanded Metropolis all over the world without ever moving out of her own locality (Warden Road to Peddar Road to Altamount Road). She went into a new business—pathology labs—just when it was taking off, but has been fortunate enough to build on her father's expertise. And though she is a successful, hardworking woman entrepreneur, she has not had to sacrifice her personal life. (Her brief marriage did not work, but she is now in a happy, stable relationship.) She was no academic genius but drew her life lessons from the things she was good at—the outdoorsy life and trekking in particular.

But there have been huge learnings. Though her parents had successful medical practices, they were professionals, not business people. Ameera has had to learn about building organisations, expanding into new markets, professionalising operations, dealing with investors and of course, how to fight a corporate war within your own corporation.

It has been difficult, she says, but not impossible. Too many women from upper middle class backgrounds (actually, why just women; it is as true for men) believe that business is a strange world that those from professional backgrounds have difficulty fitting into. It is not so difficult, she says. And she is determined to prove it. Among her initiatives is one to help female entrepreneurs and she spends several days just talking to young women who need to be mentored and seek advice. She says she learned a lot because Deepak Parekh (of HDFC) devoted time talking to her and feels that she too must share her learnings and experience with those who need it.

Ameera is forty years old. After growing a company worth thousands of crores, acquiring labs all over the world, dealing with private equity and winning a mega corporate battle within her own company, what is left for her to do?

She seems surprised by the question. She does not see this as anywhere near the high point for her career. Yes, Metropolis now has a CEO who she has enormous regard and respect for, which leaves her free to look at the big picture, and yes, there are no more tensions within the company.

But there is still a long way for Metropolis to grow, both here and abroad. She believes that the company has only just begun to operate at peak efficiency and believes that its best years are still ahead of it.

Is she surprised by how things have turned out? Did she ever think, when she was the sporty daughter of doctor parents, that she would be worth thousands of crores one day?

Well, she says, the money doesn't matter that much. She recognises that she is rich but she is not into things. Her clothes are still high street rather than designer. Her flat on Altamount Road is rented. And except for the freedom to travel where and when she wants to, she doesn't really make much of the money.

But as far as the success goes, you get the sense that as much as she enjoys it, she is not particularly surprised by how well she has done.

After all, Ameera Shah has never been short on imagination. Or confidence.

SAMEER SAIN

If you have never heard of Sameer Sain, don't worry. That's the way he likes it. The chances are, however, that you will have heard of some of the food and beverage ventures he has either invested in or owned: Burger King (India), Farzi Cafe, Masala Library, Coffee Bean & Tea Leaf, Modern Bread, Sula Wines and so many more.

Many people in the F&B business think that this is his primary activity. And he is content to let them think that. In reality, of course, his large investments in F&B across the world (Duck & Rice in London, Dominos and Burger King in Indonesia, Harry's in Singapore, etc.) actually form a tiny part of his portfolio and activities. His biggest play may well be a business called IndoSpace, which is one of India's largest real estate developers and the leader in logistics and warehousing, a distinctly unglamorous sector where he is the key player. Right after closing a 1.2 billion dollar deal with the Canadian Pension Plan for his industrial assets—one of the largest investments ever made in the Indian Real Estate space—he has just signed another one billion dollar Joint Venture with GLP for their entry into the Indian market. A marquis transaction where the global leader in Industrial and Logistics Real Estate

(GLP) partners with the local leader (IndoSpace) with Sain continuing to retain control of the venture.

The Everstone Group, the business Sain founded with his friend, Atul Kapur, now has assets of over five billion and employs over 1,00,000 people—and the founders are millionaires many times over.

Sameer Sain is unusual for many reasons. First of all, even though he was not born into a business family, he demonstrated entrepreneurial instincts even while he was a teenager. Second, when he was already making millions working for Goldman Sachs in London at the age of thirty-five, he threw it all away, liquidated his assets and transferred almost all of his money to India officially and converted them to rupees. He fought his family who didn't want him to quit his lucrative job and shake up their then perfect life. But Sain went ahead anyway because he believed that his future lay in his own country.

Third, he created the Everstone billions, almost from scratch. An early partnership with the Future Group did not work out. Sain, who was anyway considered a newcomer to Indian business, was regarded as a goner by most of the investment and business community. But, within a year he bounced back and built a formidable business despite having none of the advantages necessary to succeed in India: no family name or connections, no prestigious corporate tie-up and no favours from anyone.

And finally, he is unusual because he did it on his own terms. No black money, no bribing, no cutting corners and no making excuses ('This is how business is done in India') for unethical behaviour. Just pure passion, determination and a lot of resilience.

The Sameer Sain story starts in Landmark, an apartment building on Carter Road in the Mumbai suburb of Bandra where Sain's parents lived. His father, a textile engineer held a senior position with the government-owned National Textile Corporation. As Sain and his sister grew up, they had the perks of then government servants: chauffeured cars, holidays in guest houses, status, etc. But they never had excess money, given that government salaries were pitifully low.

None of this mattered to the young Sameer. As he recalls it, he was a strange child, both aggressively inquisitive and destructive at the same time. Show him a gadget and he would break it to see what was inside or to figure out how it worked. He smoked weed, wrote poetry, played cricket and listened obsessively to the Doors. He didn't seem particularly connected to anyone or anything and had a very short attention span (a trait his friends and colleagues will vouch for even today). He jokingly says that had he grown up in America, instead of the occasional whack on the head, he would have probably been diagnosed with Attention Deficient Syndrome.

After finishing his ICSE at Jamnabai Narsee School, his parents sent him to Mumbai's well-respected Sydenham College but that kind of archaic theoretical 'mugging' education bored him. So, by the time he was eighteen, he had already figured out a way to trade in the chemicals required by the textile industry.

He was good at it; he worked out how to turn a profit, given the difference between his cost price and the rates he knew the products were being sold for. But he had reckoned without the corruption that is endemic to Indian business.

Everywhere he tried, they were willing to buy his product. But the purchase manager, the quality control guys and executives at various levels all demanded kickbacks. When Sameer refused to pay them off, his products were rejected on 'quality grounds' and the contracts fell through.

The experience left him with a deep and abiding contempt for the way business was done in India in the 1980s. And he developed a new obsession: going abroad to study.

His father and he could probably find the money for the course between them. But there was another problem. Sain had no postgraduate degree. He had no American-style qualifications (no SAT, TOEFL or anything like that). So, naturally, college after college turned down his application.

'The story of my life,' he says, 'is that I am usually rejected the first time I try for something. And then I make it happen anyway. I love being the underdog and have gotten used to being consistently written off and underestimated.' So it was with this admission that he started making phone calls to Deans of American colleges. And nobody took his call.

But he didn't give up. Finally, the Dean of the University of Massachusetts at Amherst agreed to talk to him. Sameer is still not sure of what he did right in that conversation but the Dean agreed to waive the rules, make an exception and accept him. Moreover, Sain would get two years credit for the time he had spent at Sydenham from where he got his B.Com degree.

For Sain, like many upper middle class kids of his generation, America was the promised land not because it guaranteed success but because so many of the cultural reference points back in Bandra had been American: from the movies to the books to the music.

So, he had no difficulty fitting in when he got to college. But he discovered that business studies was the most boring subject he had ever come across. So despite having got in to study business, he took all the liberal arts courses that he could find, refined his love for poetry and—'Let's be honest,'—spent a lot of his time 'partying like crazy. I had multiple jobs to support my lifestyle—waiter, bartender, resident assistant—one summer I even cleaned mouldy refrigerators to pay off the credit card bills. But I look back and I actually enjoyed all of these jobs and remember having fun and doing them with passion!'

By the time his undergraduate course was coming to an end, it was time to apply for an MBA. He did this methodically choosing the five top business schools and applying to five lesser places as a back-up.

He got a rude shock when all five of his back-up colleges took almost no time to reject him. His lack of work experience and young age went against him!

Recognising that the top colleges were certain to do the same, Sameer rented a car and drove to all five of them. He decided he would do what he always does best: make a passionate plea to the admissions officers and convince them to give him a chance. He insisted they interview him before they made a decision.

Bizarrely, all five accepted him. He says, 'I was getting good at this but I knew in my heart that I truly deserved that chance,' he quips. He chose Cornell in upstate New York but once he got there, he realised that studying business was still boring. So he took every non-business course he could find, including many at the prestigious Cornell Hotel School which inculcated in him a lifelong love of food and wine.

Cornell was great. But as all business students know, it is the next step that is important: where you end up as a summer intern. He knew that being one of the youngest in his class with no prior work experience would be a big stumbling block in his quest for a summer job.

Sain had always been clear about where he wanted to work: McKinsey, the management consultancy giant. But as was the pattern in his life, McKinsey turned him down at the first interview itself.

That left Goldman Sachs, then as now, the world's most powerful investment bank or, as the critics call it, the giant vampire squid wrapped around the face of the world's economy.

Sameer somehow managed to get an on-campus interview with Goldman. But Sain did not have a suit to wear to the interview. Nor could he afford one. So he called his father who promised to courier one to him. When it arrived, Sameer was pleased to see that it came from Kachins, a famous Mumbai tailor of that era, but appalled to discover that it was olive green. His father, unused to the ways of Wall Street, had decided that green was a stylish colour.

The interview did not go well. Not because Sain spoke badly, but because his qualifications were not good enough for that supremely competitive job. The interviewer, a successful woman, was particularly aggressive with him and felt he was wasting his time. Recognising that things were going poorly, Sain took a chance.

He revealed to the interviewer that he had been warned that she had a reputation of being unpleasant and that he was sorry to see it was true.

All human beings have their frailties, sometimes when you least expect them to. 'Who told you that?' the Goldman interviewer asked, genuinely concerned. 'Who said I was not a nice person? I'm just trying to do my job,' she said.

Sain had his opening and he used it. Finally, after listening to him, the now somewhat discomfited interviewer told him that there was still no way she could select him. His lack of experience still remained a problem.

But there was a chance. She gave him a clue. If he called a man named Alok Oberoi, a Senior Director at Goldman Sachs in London, perhaps he could help. Oberoi was Indian and had also studied at Cornell. So, there was some meeting ground. She wished him luck and left.

Easier said than done. Sain kept calling Oberoi in London only to find himself blocked by his secretary. He gets forty calls a day from people like you, she told Sameer. He is not going to talk to you.

By then Sain had started to recognise the pattern of consistently being rejected the first time but had also become convinced of his ability to be persistent and resilient. He called every day for several weeks.

Finally, the secretary took pity on him. 'Look,' she told Sain, 'I'm not allowed to put through calls from guys like you. But I come to work at 8.30 a.m. everyday. He comes in at 8 a.m., and for the half hour before I come in, he answers his own phone. I'm not saying it will work. But your best chance is to call him between 8 and 8.30 a.m.'

This was all London time of course and Ithaca, New York, was five hours behind. But Sain stayed up and made the call anyway in the early hours of the American morning. As predicted, Oberoi answered his own phone. But when Sain began his pitch, Oberoi cut him off.

'Just give me a minute,' Sameer pleaded.

'I don't work like that,' Oberoi told him. 'I need to see a resume.'

'Give me a number,' Sain persisted. 'I'll fax it to you.'

Perhaps only to get him off the phone, Oberoi gave him a fax number.

At this stage it was the height of the American winter and early morning in Ithaca. Sain wrapped himself warmly, shovelled the snow away from his car and went off to a 'Open 24 hours' Kinkos and faxed his resume.

He called Oberoi soon after.

'Did you get it?' he asked.

'Yes,' said Oberoi. 'I'm looking at it now and it does not seem very impressive.... Hang on a minute. Where are you?'

'At Cornell. In Ithaca,' Sain told him.

'You have a fax machine at home?'

'No, I went to the Kinkos in Ithaca.'

'What time is it there?'

'It's 4 a.m.,' quipped Sain.

'What's the temperature?'

'It's freezing. Minus something.'

Oberoi was impressed. Being very familiar with Ithaca winters, he could relate to the commitment shown by Sain. Okay, he said. He would arrange an interview with a partner at Goldman Sachs over video conferencing. But Sain would have to prove himself.

So, many days later, Sain found himself in the New York offices of Goldman Sachs on a video conference with Dr Joseph Sassoon, a senior partner at Goldman Sachs, London.

As always, he talked his way through the interview. But Sassoon, a skeptical PhD from Oxford, did not seem convinced.

'It says on your resume,' he told Sain, 'that you read and write poetry. Recite one of the first poems you wrote.'

And so shyly, awkwardly, Sain gathered his thoughts. He wrote down a few lines on a paper in front of him and recited a short quartet.

Sassoon smiled. Something about this young kid's confidence and personality appealed to him. He decided to take a chance and Sain was taken on as a summer intern.

Most people who join a brokerage firm or an investment bank are awed by the scale of the operation they have become part of. They are particularly intimidated by the noise and sheer power of the trading floor where deals worth millions of dollars are struck every second.

Not Sameer Sain.

'It was a mad jungle,' he recalls. 'And I knew I was home. For some reason I found that I think better with chaos around me.'

The curious, destructive, impatient, aggressive boy had finally found the habitat he was meant to roam. Like some animal born into the wrong environment and unable to fit in, Sain suddenly discovered the jungle he should have been born into, the place where he belonged.

Most people die in the jungle that is the trading floor. A few survive. But only a tiny proportion flourish. Sain made the floor his own proving ground. Interns like him were only meant to get coffee for traders. But he managed to execute trades himself and because he showed such flair and no fear, the experienced traders took to him.

When the work experience period was over, Goldman told most of the interns to go home. A chosen few—Sameer Sain, among them—were told they could come back and become full-fledged employees.

By then, almost everybody there had guessed what would happen. Sameer proved to be a natural. He was so good at making money for Goldman that they made him an Executive Director in London. Within a few years of joining, he was making over a million dollars himself. He bought a new house, a Porsche and lived the high-pressure and high-maintenance life.

But somehow, it always nagged him that no matter how well he did, he would always be regarded as an outsider, an Indian. Often when new opportunities in Europe were being discussed, he was told, 'That's a great idea. But Sameer, we are not sure this is for you.'

So Sameer began thinking beyond Europe. One morning at a routine meeting at the office, he was asked what new business ideas he had. Sameer said, just for the heck of it, 'Kenya.'

'Kenya?'

'Yeah!'

'You sure?'

'Yeah. It's a huge opportunity for us.'

In truth, Sameer Sain knew nothing about Kenya. He mentioned it because by then, he was just so pissed off about not being given what he felt were the best-suited European opportunities, and he knew there were many Indians in Kenya!

'Okay, Sameer,' they told him. 'You go to Nairobi and handle it.'

Sain flew into the Kenyan capital not knowing what he would find. He checked into Nairobi's best hotel, went through the phone book and called the first Patel he found.

That Mr Patel turned out to be the owner of a toyshop with only a dim idea of what Goldman Sachs was. But he gave Sain the names of the richest Indians in Nairobi.

Sameer called them. And they certainly had heard of Goldman Sachs. Within three years, Goldman had a business worth several hundred million dollars out of Kenya.

'Water will always find a way if you just let it flow,' he says.

There were other irritants too. He went on holiday to the Algarve in Portugal having secured the requisite visa. He flew business class and after landing found himself at the head of the immigration queue.

The officer took one look at his passport, looked up at Sameer and in a harsh tone said, 'Indian? Ok, you wait in the corner.'

And so Sameer had to sit on the side. When the officer had finished waving by all the passengers, he called Sameer to his desk, asked him a few questions and finally stamped his passport and allowed him in.

For Sameer, the humiliation set something off. While he was eligible for other citizenships he always held on to his Indian passport. Finally, he said to himself, 'enough is enough.' He was entitled to a British passport by virtue of residence so he got himself one.

But it never really felt right. One summer afternoon, he was driving through the Strand in London when his car (a luxury convertible, of course) stopped at a traffic light. Two white British men in suits emerged from a pub, probably a little drunk.

One of them stopped, turned in Sain's direction and yelled. 'You, fucking Paki. Go back to where you come from.'

By this stage, Sain was so used to being a successful part of the London financial establishment that he looked back to see who it was the guy was yelling at.

When he finally realised that he was the target of the abuse, he was truly shocked.

'You know, I thought to myself,' he recalls, 'I've probably paid more in taxes in the last year than this asshole earned in total over the last ten years.'

He was almost certainly right. Despite being successful and by now running an important part of Goldman's European business as a Managing Director, he was still a 'Paki' in somebody else's country.

It was experiences like these that convinced Sameer Sain that his place was back home and one day he woke up and his mind was made up. He was going to go back to India.

He could, possibly, have done it with Goldman. Some years before, he had accompanied Hank Paulson, then a top gun at Goldman, on a trip to check out opportunities in

India. The trip had gone well but Paulson was not pleased. He had enthusiastically attended a puja in his socks, only to find, when the puja was over, that somebody had stolen one of his shoes. Legend has it that Paulson swore there and then never to return to India, a vow he kept till he became US Treasury Secretary.

But by now, Sain was tired of working for foreign firms. He wanted to come back to India and start something of his own.

Enter Kishore Biyani of the Future group (then just Pantaloon Retail), an old family friend. Biyani offered to partner with him to start a new financial services venture.

Sain agreed and moved back to India to create and lead this new venture called Future Capital. They incorporated and funded the company together and each took their proportionate share but with Sain as MD&CEO. Sain was clear from day one that he would not accept any free equity or shares. At first, things went swimmingly well. Biyani and Sain were very different but they made a good team. The venture was a success, they took it public and both parties ended up with shares worth hundreds of crores.

But slowly the differences of approach and style became more apparent and started to cause minor friction. Eventually says Sain, he went to Biyani and told him, 'This is not working as we envisaged and we both know this could lead to issues between us down the road. Better we part today as friends.'

Biyani agreed. Their mutual respect and friendship allowed for an amicable separation, but most people wrote off Sain as having little chance of survival without Kishore as his partner.

But Sain found a new partner in Atul Kapur and started Everstone. Sain knew that appearances count for a lot in the financial world, so even though Everstone was cash-poor, he spent lavishly on new offices and acted as though nothing had changed. 'In order to be successful, I had to feel successful and then let reality catch up. Strangely I am most optimistic when I'm down and tend to get skeptical when I am on top,' he recalls. 'In order to be successful, I had to feel successful and then let reality catch up,' he recalls. Slowly, he sold his shares in Future Capital and added the crores to the Everstone equity base. Other investors trusted Kapur and him and invested hundreds of millions of dollars in them.

Today, Everstone has over five billion dollars in equity assets alone. It is so cash-rich that even big businessmen look to Sain and Kapur for funding and the company is a dream investor for any start-up. In addition to being a leading private equity investor, Everstone has also built one of India's largest real estate developers (IndoSpace); a highly successful venture business with their partner Deepak Shahdadpuri (DSG); and one of the finest and most successful Non Bank Finance Companies (NBFC) called Indostar. All this was created from scratch. Most recently, the Indian and UK governments partnered and jointly trusted Everstone with a seed corpus of 2,200 crores to invest in and build green infrastructure in India under a partnership called Eversource (a joint venture between Everstone and BP Lightsource).

In a sense, Sain has lived two distinct lives. In many ways, he is still the same man: he worships Jim Morrison and the Doors; he can still get the measure of a man in a few minutes; and he can also passionately connect with people at almost any level.

But he is not a Wall Street-style Master of the Universe. Rather, he has to contend with the rough and tumble of Indian business.

I asked him what the differences between his two lives were.

'It all boils down to a few basic observations and principles. For one, many Indian businesses have gotten used to focusing on what they can do rather than what they should do. At some level I understand this. So many archaic laws and such a volatile environment creates acute short term and opportunistic thinking.

'You would think,' he continues, 'this is not really in their interests. They should do the rational thing and try to think long-term. Therefore, I have learned to never try and predict someone's behaviour or what they will do; instead I merely observe what they actually do and assess all the possible options of what they can do. Talk is cheap and very distracting. Once you cut out all the noise, only then you can truly understand the environment.'

I don't disagree with him but that leads to the next question. How does Everstone continue to flourish in this environment despite Sain's oft-repeated refrain that they will function ethically and never deal in black money?

'You can, you know,' he says. 'Sometimes not coming from a business family and working for a good company for many years before you become an entrepreneur can be an advantage—you just don't know any other way! There are enough such role models in our country. People like taking short-cuts. It's much easier in the short term because you don't really compete on a level playing field. But in the long run, all this gets exposed. I believe the generation of today understands this and wants to do things the right way. I don't care to preach, but the truth is there is no substitute for obsessive passion and persistence. I also think the environment and policies are changing, slowly but surely. We are still a young country. America in its first hundred years as a nation went through its motions to get there as well. We forget all the Wild West and mafia movies. But there was still room for so many amazing entrepreneurs who did things the right way. We will get there as well.'

Doesn't that pose problems for a firm that wants to function ethically today? 'Yes, it does,' he concedes. 'People hate it when you stand up to them and refuse to be slapped around. You have to be strong and resilient. But you also got to realise that, at the end of the day, the biggest bullies are also the biggest cowards. They will threaten you and try to scare you but if you stand strong and consistent, you will prevail. If I had a dollar for every time that someone said to me, "You don't know who I am," or "Just watch what I will do to you," I would be an extremely rich man!'

Ignoring the fact that he is a rich man anyway, I ask if these threats faze him. 'They used to,' he admits. 'But only in the beginning. In the long run, nobody can really damage you if you are innocent and haven't done anything wrong. They may be able to intimidate you but we do live in a democratic country with rules and laws and, while it may take time and patience, you have to believe that eventually justice does prevail. So now, when people threaten me and brag about their power and their contacts, I just tell them, "Do whatever you like." I stick to my style and principles. If you are doing things the right way then there is no reason to be afraid.

'The last thing I will say is never be scared of becoming an entrepreneur, or a businessman as most people say. I've realised that the really bright people in our country are not entrepreneurs, they are mostly in simple jobs—employed by someone else. They aspire to be good professionals. They think, "We are not from a business family" or, "It's such a difficult and dirty world." There is a combination of fear and stigma. So the guys who used to go into business—maybe its changing now—are not always the brightest guys, but those who had the advantage of being born into business families, or thinking that they knew how to game the system.

'But I think that is changing. The new business leaders of this country will be entrepreneurs who will emerge from "service-class" families. Using a cricketing analogy, if we always believed that in order to really succeed in cricket and play at the highest level you have to hail from the elite Mumbai or Delhi clubs and colleges, then we would never have a Dhoni. But to be a Dhoni, you have to have tons of passion, be very persistent but most importantly, stick to your style and principles. The problem lies with our aspirations. I truly hope for an India where parents wish for their children to be entrepreneurs rather than to merely pray they get a good and stable job!'

After several years in Mumbai (in Bandra but in a fancier building than Carter Road's Landmark) Sain has moved to Singapore as his business has expanded into other parts of Asia and the US. But he spends over one-third of each month in India, checking out new opportunities and overseeing his existing businesses.

Is it possible, I ask him, for an investor with so many varied interests and businesses to really understand them all?

He is candid: no, it is not. 'The trick is to hire people or, at least, to trust people who know what they are doing. It's all about having the right talent. I believe my job is to harness the passion and entrepreneurial spirit of talented people and share the upside with them. All you have to do is to know enough to make yourself dangerous!'

So how much does he know? I take the example of Burger King, which now has over 200 outlets in India within five years and is still growing.

'Which outlet do you want to know about?' he asks. 'Saket?'

I say yes. It is the one outlet I had been to. He pulls up his phone and presses a few buttons.

'Ok,' he says. 'This is Saket today. I can show you the total sales so far. I can show you the difference over this day last week.' He clicks around a little more.

'These are the menu items that have moved today. This is the list of bills the cashiers have rung up today. You will see how Sunil (I've changed the names of the cashiers) has had an average check size of 240 rupees while Anchan has rung up only 160 rupees. So Anchan will go back into training. He has to learn to up-sell at the till.'

So, is all this on his smartphone at any given time?

'Yes. But I don't call up every day. Once a month, when I have a review meeting with the management team, I listen. I have the best CEO for this business who is a fellow shareholder as well. I don't need to second guess him. Usually, my team would have picked up on all the trends. But if they have not, then I know enough to be dangerous and push their thinking,' he smiles, a little mirthlessly.

How does a guy who abandoned the Wall Street/City of London lifestyle to move back to India, now see himself?

'Oh, I am a global Indian,' he says. 'There are so many of us. The world still thinks: he is an Indian, what does he know? But the truth is: we know a lot and we are not afraid.'

Warming to his theme, he continues, 'When you have enough skill and experience, you can play each ball on its merit. For example, if someone wants to engage me on French wine or American contemporary art, I'm very curious and keen to learn, provided they know the subject or have an interesting perspective. But I won't be lectured-to or talked-down simply because I'm Indian and therefore they assume I don't know shit.'

In fact, I've met very few people who know as much about fine wine as Sain. Most of us who talk about wine, read about it. But Sain not only reads about it, he actually drinks the world's finest wines and knows many of the winemakers personally. The same can be said for his taste in art.

'I think a new kind of global Indian is emerging,' he says. 'We have knowledge, experience and passion and we do not get intimidated. We are proud of our heritage and we resent the suggestion that because we are Indians we are at a disadvantage to anyone or on any issue. We are confident, curious and ready to engage.'

Sain is still only forty-eight. Success has come early to him. So has he made enough money?

'What's enough! Yes, more than enough to live. But that's not the point. Money alone is never the point. Even when I had very little money, I lived like I had enough. Money is just a score, kind of like runs for a batsman. It's important, but the true joy is to play the game at the highest level, enjoy the journey and occasionally surprise everyone with winning as an underdog like we did in the 1983 Cricket World Cup! Besides, I have a huge fiduciary responsibility to those who have invested with me, my team and my various stakeholders. I take great joy and pride in making money for them. Only then am I content to make money for myself. There is also a feeling of pride when I see the number of jobs we have created and the value we have added with all our new businesses and investments. There is no price for this!'

So, what's left?

'Well, I have a couple of big business ideas I will unleash soon, but I also have many other interests. I want to make a hard-hitting documentary. I want to record a music album, I want to write a book. I have so many interests from contemporary art to wine to children's education. I want our philanthropic arm (Everstone Foundation) to be our biggest venture yet. And that is all without compromising my business goals. There is so much to experience. I feel I'm just getting started.'

This is not a man with a limited range of ambitions. He wants it all. He's got most of it, already.

And he always knows enough about everything to be dangerous.

ARNAB GOSWAMI

Many Indians of a certain generation believe that Arnab Goswami invented news television. Their reasoning is straightforward enough: not only is he the most famous and most watched anchor on English language TV in India, nearly everybody else on the news, on every channel, is an Arnab-clone of one sort or another. So, they reckon, Arnab must have invented the genre.

Well, yes and no. There has always been news TV in India. Even in its earliest days, Doordarshan had a news division with presenters (or 'newsreaders' as we called them in that era), who became household names. And then, when the State broadcaster opened its doors to private producers, new celebrities emerged. Prannoy Roy of NDTV, the company he owned and ran with his wife, Radhika Roy, became one on Doordarshan before shifting to Star TV. When Star wanted to start a news channel, they called it Star News but allowed NDTV to run it. S.P. Singh, a former print editor, fronted a news show called Aaj Tak on Doordarshan. The show was produced by the India Today group, which eventually used the name to launch one of India's top Hindi news channels.

As the private news channels flourished, so did the top anchors, men and women like Rajat Sharma, Rajdeep Sardesai,

Barkha Dutt, Ravish Kumar, Vinod Dua and many others. All became stars, though obviously, some shone brighter than others.

But, to begin with, Arnab Goswami was not one of them. And as the TV boom started, Goswami watched it from the sidelines, not even sure that he wanted to become a journalist, let alone a television anchor.

Arnab Goswami comes from a family with a long tradition of intellectual achievement and some political involvement. An ancestor was one of the founders of the Communist Party of India. Another relative was part of the Congress, and other members of the family have contested elections on behalf of many political parties including the BJP.

So the home that Arnab grew up in was no stranger to political discussion, though his own father was in the Indian army. Because his father was transferred all around India, Arnab attended schools in many cities, most of which he remembers with affection.

They were always comfortably off though like all army families, there was never much cash. Instead, intellectual accomplishment became the family's wealth.

Arnab was admitted into Delhi's Hindu College (rather than the tonier St. Stephen's, which has been a breeding ground for many Delhi journalists) and studied Sociology, giving no real thought to the career he wanted to follow. Though he shies away from saying it himself, he must have been academically gifted because he was confident enough to apply to Oxford University to read Social Anthropology at St. Antony's, a high-brow college noted for its postgraduate teaching. When the admission came through, he had no money to pay for the course and went looking for scholarships.

In his telling, he was pretty much the average bookish student in those days. But this can't have been entirely true. At one scholarship interview, he came up against the legendary Ranjit Bhatia, a don at St. Stephen's who was on virtually every scholarship committee (Rhodes, Inlaks, etc.) in Delhi.

Bhatia asked him, in the course of the interview, why he believed he was deserving of the scholarship.

'Because I am not from St. Stephen's College,' Arnab responded, a little defiantly.

Bhatia was taken aback and sought him out after the interview. 'Young man,' he told him 'you mustn't think that we are biased towards St. Stephen's students...'

Arnab recalls the incident even now and though he is not sure what led to that little flash of defiance (and perhaps, to a foretaste of the Arnab to come), he remembers Bhatia fondly. 'He was a very nice man,' he says.

Of course, he got the scholarship, and landed up at St. Antony's where the average age of the students was in their Thirties (Arnab was only twenty-one). He enjoyed the opportunity to discuss Social Anthropology with some of Oxford's finest minds, earned a postgraduate degree and came back to India, confident that he could pursue a career in academics.

Nevertheless, he checked out his options. He was offered a job by IPAN, the PR company, but was encouraged to seek a different path by the journalist Chandan Mitra who told him he wrote well and sent him off to see Swapan Dasgupta who was then editing the *Indian Express'* opinion pages. Dasgupta suggested he move to Calcutta where the *Telegraph* was looking for people to work on the editorials.

Arnab liked the idea, took the *Telegraph* job and worked on the edit page for nine months, editing copy, handling production and writing non-stop (he probably wrote around seventy pieces in those nine months).

But he still wasn't sure what he wanted to do and so when NDTV came looking for staff in Calcutta in 1995, Arnab attended the interviews at the Peerless Hotel, was auditioned by the late K.V.L. Narayan Rao (who headed the management side of what was then a small company) and hired.

In those days, there was no 24-hour news channels. NDTV made shows for Doordarshan and other channels. Arnab reported and anchored bulletins and a variety of programmes. The experience interested him, he says, because he had not entered journalism through the usual route (starting out as a reporter) and felt that he needed to learn ground-level reporting.

He put his heart and soul into it, making connections on all his beats. For instance, he says, he knew three different ways into the CBI building and had developed contacts at every level of the organisation, starting from the top with the then Director, Joginder Singh. His willingness to sweat it out did not go unnoticed. On one occasion, he stood with a crew outside L.K. Advani's house from morning till evening. In that time, Advani came and left his house several times. Presumably he noticed Arnab because, at the end of the day, he was intrigued enough to call the crew in and commend Arnab for his persistence.

Eventually NDTV ran the Star News channel for Star TV. And in the era of 24-hour news TV, Arnab flourished. He anchored the long-running two-presenter daily news and analysis show and became one of the channel's best-known faces.

But something did not feel right. His academic background kept his brain ticking away and he began to form strong views on several subjects, including national security and terrorism.

Finally, Arnab asked to see his NDTV boss, Prannoy Roy and told him that he needed a sabbatical.

Roy agreed and Arnab went off to Cambridge where he was one of the youngest Visiting Fellows at Sidney Sussex College. A book on terrorism and how to handle it (*Combating Terrorism: The Legal Challenge*) emerged out of that stint and though this was not immediately apparent to viewers of NDTV, many of the hardline views that are now associated with Arnab had already begun to coalesce by 2000-2001.

NDTV has always been one of India's most extraordinary media companies. Founded by the Roys, who continue to manage it, the organisation marked a break with the old-style media company where there was a clear divide between the (usually dynastic) owners and the editorial staff. Because the Roys had created the company themselves only on the basis of their own talent and skills, they felt a greater empathy with the journalists and worked closely with them, offering a more equal relationship than the old-style proprietors.

Their approach was benevolent and paternalistic (sometimes, literally: they functioned as surrogate parents for some of their employees) and the Roys personally mentored the young journalists they believed would become stars. (In nearly every case, their instincts were spot on.)

Arnab got along with the Roys. To this day, he has nothing but praise for them. But he was never a particular favourite and there seems to have been no special personal relationship.

Nor was he especially matey with the channel's star anchors. There is a famous (though possibly apocryphal) NDTV story, still retold by harried producers, about a two-anchor programme where Barkha Dutt, his co-anchor, smiled a lot but refused to read out any of her links from the teleprompter.

Apparently, she felt that as Arnab liked talking so much, he might as well have the whole show to himself.

By 2002, two years after the Roys split with Star and renamed their channel, NDTV 24x7, there was already a sense that anybody from the team who went off and started a competing channel could give NDTV a run for its money. NDTV's biggest star, Rajdeep Sardesai, left to team up with Raghav Bahl to start CNN-IBN (now CNN-News 18). Arnab says he also felt the urge to leave and do something on his own.

That opportunity came when the *Times of India* called. The Times Group ran three of India's most successful newspapers but believed, reasonably enough, that it was time to diversify into other media. The problem was that the group's first TV channel, Zoom, had bombed and the Times was not sure what to do next. A news channel in English seemed like a safe bet and they tapped Arnab to run it.

We think of Times Now as an instant success. In fact, it was nothing of the sort. When they hired Arnab, the *Times of India's* managers had only thought vaguely of an NDTV-type channel that reflected the print edition's content.

When Arnab came in, he realised that the venture needed more money than the Times had recognised, so he actively courted the Reuters news agency, making trips abroad (along with the management team) to persuade Reuters to invest in the news channel. But even then, the vision was of an all-round channel, a little like CNN International perhaps, with news, sport and business on weekdays, and programming on weekends.

The main news show anchored by Arnab, would be a two-presenter show, like the NDTV shows that had made Arnab's reputation. And because the Times liked boasting about the difference between news and views, there would be no editorialising, at all.

The channel took a while to get started and it launched after Sardesai's CNN-IBN had already shown that NDTV could be challenged by a newer version of itself. With NDTV and CNN-IBN going head to head, it was hard to find compelling reasons to watch a third channel, also run by an ex-NDTV face which offered yet another version of the same format.

By 2007, over a year after Times Now had begun telecasting, Arnab knew they were in trouble. There was nothing wrong with their shows—the flagship programme, the Newshour, presented by Arnab and Mini Menon (who he praises for her anchoring skills) was fine—but the channel just did not seem different enough or even, particularly special. Why would you watch Times Now when you already had enough of this stuff on NDTV and CNN-IBN?

Everyone is broadly agreed that the Times Now we know was created around 2008-2009. The dispute is over how that change came about. One explanation is that the Times Group looked at the American market, saw that Fox News was beating CNN, and decided that the same model could work here.

Nobody within the Times buys this version. The Fox News parallels, they say, came much after the event, and were made by others. Arnab—and his Times bosses—had never watched much of Fox News.

A second version is that the 26/11 Mumbai attacks were the turning point. This story, at least, has some semblance of the truth. Certainly Times Now did the best 26/11 coverage. Unlike NDTV and CNN-IBN, which are Delhi-based, Times Now is headquartered in Mumbai so the attacks were a local story for the channel. Perhaps as a consequence, Times Now had the most exhaustive reporting on the attacks.

Arnab despatched reporters and anchors to the scenes of the terror and spent almost the entire duration of the siege behind his desk, seeming to need no sleep or, for that matter, any loo breaks.

Much of the time, his face was not on the air. But as the channel ran footage from all over Mumbai, he offered a non-stop audio commentary from behind his desk.

After 26/11, nobody took Times Now for granted. It had done a much better job than either NDTV or CNN-IBN.

But this single incident does not explain how the channel suddenly leapfrogged ahead of its rivals and became India's number one TV station for English news.

There is, in fact, a third explanation.

With the channel flailing and the ratings in free fall, Arnab took a decision to drastically revamp the format. Out went all the expensive weekend programming. Out went business, glamour and all the other non-political stuff. There were to be no high-priced hirings of big-name anchors. Money would only be spent on reporting.

All this, you could argue—as many did at the time— emerged out of his management's decision to cut costs in areas where the channel was not doing well.

But as for the change in format, well that, I think, we will have to agree, was all Arnab and only Arnab.

It is important to realise that even though he had worked hard on his reporting skills at his time at NDTV, Arnab is not your average journo. His background is academics and his intellectual skills were honed in the cut and thrust of the Oxbridge system where students are expected to take a position and to then defend it against all comers. By the time Arnab went to Cambridge for his second Oxbridge stint, he was only twenty-seven but he had already adopted strong positions on such issues as security and had defended them against some of the best minds at one of the world's greatest universities.

There are not many twenty-seven-year-olds who would feel the need to take time off from their successful careers to write academic books on terrorism and law, believing that they had something important and useful to contribute to the discourse on that subject. But Arnab has always been like that. His journalism has always emerged from his ability to categorically state—and then defend—his own position on every issue.

When he worked on the editorial page of the *Telegraph,* this was fair enough. He was an opinion writer, so the job was all about his views. But by the time he got to NDTV, he began to find the culture of enforced neutrality oppressive.

'They would always tell me: don't put your own views into the story,' he remembers. 'And I never really agreed with that. I think it was because NDTV had started out making programmes for Doordarshan that they always felt that they could not risk offending anyone.'

He was annoyed too, he recalls, by the tight format of his NDTV show. 'Everything had to be fitted into one hour. If you had guests on the show, then every conversation had to be wrapped up in fifteen or twenty minutes. And at the end of each discussion, you had to find a common ground. It was as though you couldn't allow people to express very sharp disagreements.'

He hated that culture of enforced consensus, he says. 'I have been a debater all my life, through school, college, everything. I like the idea of people disagreeing and defending their own views. Why should we make them discuss something for just fifteen minutes and then end it on a note of bogus agreement?'

There was also something of the boy who defiantly told Ranjit Bhatia that he was not from St. Stephen's, still lurking within Arnab. Though he had been well-connected in his Delhi days, he had never been a political insider in the way that some of his colleagues were. And now, operating out of a studio in Mumbai, he felt even more removed from the Delhi political-bureaucratic circuit.

'Every time we did a debate on NDTV,' he remembers, 'we would get the same kind of people. If it was a foreign policy debate, then there would be one former Foreign Secretary, one foreign policy expert from a Delhi think tank or a columnist from a newspaper; the same sort of people really. I began to question that. Why shouldn't somebody from outside that establishment also have a say?'

And so the Times Now debates began to feature people who had never been on television before and who, in most cases, viewers had never heard of. 'I found that the viewers were responsive to new faces. But it was the establishment that objected,' he says. 'I remember that right after 26/11, we invited some different voices on the show. And I began to get calls from the Foreign ministry. They would say things like, "Who are these people? How can you ask them to comment on foreign policy issues?" And I decided there and then that we would get more such non-establishment voices.'

But apart from the emphasis on debates where people disagreed strongly with each other and the decision to reach out beyond the usual suspects, there were a few other key decisions that rival channels still don't fully understand. And yet, it was those decisions that took Times Now to number one.

Until Arnab, with his Mumbai offices, came along, most English media had a Delhi focus. The editors of the *Hindustan*

Times, the *Times of India* and the *Indian Express* work out of Delhi. The three other English news channels that Arnab competed with (NDTV, CNN-IBN and Headlines Today {now, India Today Television}) were all Delhi-based. So, Delhi and its neighbouring Hindi belt states received a disproportionate share of coverage.

Arnab set out to deliberately break the stranglehold of Delhi. Whereas, in the old days, debates or discussions had been largely studio-based (and therefore, dependent on Delhi guests) with the odd guest joining from out of the studio via a link, Arnab set out to find guests from all over India, especially the south.

Instead of the usual long shots of a Delhi studio where anchors chatted to guests, Arnab filled the Times Now screen with little windows in which his guests appeared. Once each guest had his or her window, it did not matter whether the guest was joining the debate from Chennai or Chandigarh. The window had become a great equaliser.

While the English channels are Delhi-centric, the ratings are national. Such English-speaking markets as Mumbai, Bengaluru and Chennai can make or break an English news channel's fortunes. Arnab reached out to these markets before his rivals did. He dealt with their concerns in his debates and featured their local celebrities in his windows.

Even when it comes to the Delhi and north India market, English channels often get it wrong. The truth is that the size of the English news audience is tiny. It hovers at around 0.4 per cent of the total television universe. While entertainment will always be more popular than news, Hindi news fares far better than English when it comes to the size of the audience. There are many days when more people watch a single Hindi news channel than all the English news channels put together.

These figures are no secret. But English news channels don't know what to make of them. Nor do they understand the sensibility of the Hindi TV viewer. When NDTV launched NDTV India and CNN-IBN ran the Hindi IBN-7, neither channel could gain much viewership.

Arnab is not a native Hindi speaker (they spoke Assamese at home when he was growing up) but the years in north Indian towns during his father's postings and his time at Hindu College gave him a certain fluency in the language.

When he recast Times Now, he recognised that the so-called Delhi and north India focus of most English channels never went beyond a narrow, well-educated band at the top of the market. The real audience consisted of those who understood English but were more comfortable watching a Hindi channel.

What if he could create an English channel which would allow Hindi-speaking guests to join its debates with an anchor who would respond to them in Hindi? What if the anchor would be happy continuing the debate in Hindi without the obvious reluctance and discomfort of the anchors on other English channels?

It was an idea whose time had come. By expanding the debaters' list to include guests from southern and eastern India, and by appealing to those north Indians who were not very comfortable with English, Times Now did what no other TV channel had done. Not only did the programmes seem different but Arnab was also able to suggest, through form and substance, that Times Now was less elitist and much more inclusive than other English channels.

As a ratings strategy, it was unbeatable. If you can win away even a small proportion of the audience that normally watches Hindi channels, then you are already way ahead of every other English channel.

Rivals on other channels who dismiss Arnab as the ringmaster of a circus of little-known debaters who shout and snarl from their windows, miss his essential shrewdness.

In an era when people can get all the news they need from their mobile phones, they will only watch TV if it engages them. So yes, they may enjoy loud raucous debates. But if the debate is about a subject that does not interest them, they will switch to an entertainment channel.

Arnab's special talent is his gut feel for the issues that will engage his audience. During UPA II, when anger against the government's perceived elitism and corruption was at its height (and Anna Hazare was elevated to instant mahatma status), Arnab hammered away at the UPA government's lack of integrity night after night.

Unlike his rivals who followed the tried-and-tested formula of getting a BJP spokesman to disagree with a Congress spokesman, while one or two 'neutral' experts made squawking noises, Arnab prefaced each debate with a revelation or a 'newsbreak'.

So, while anchors on other channels were sincerely debating the excessive expenditure incurred on hosting the Commonwealth Games in 2010, Arnab always had a 'newsbreak' to set the agenda for the angry debate that would follow: Times Now had tracked down the details of Suresh Kalmadi's latest scam! Its reporters had filed an expose from London! Why wouldn't Kalmadi comment? What was he afraid of? Did he not know that nobody could hide from Times Now? And so on.

His rivals argued angrily that many of these 'scoops' were already in the public domain (Not necessarily true. Times Now did break many stories during that period.) But what was important was this: his viewers believed that only Arnab was out there, slashing away at the old elites and fighting battles on their behalf. His readiness to abandon the role of neutral anchor and to put his own views out there further endeared him to his core viewer.

As each scandal (2G, Coalgate, etc.) came and went, Arnab grew in stature—and in popularity.

What galls Arnab's rivals most is that even though they like to portray him as a vulgarian with a manufactured disdain for the establishment, he knows exactly how to get right to the very heart of the establishment.

When Times Now secured access to the BJP leadership in 2013-2014, his competitors sneered that this was only to be expected given that Arnab had been so critical of the ruling UPA. But then, to the horror of the rest of the TV industry, Arnab secured the one interview that everybody wanted. And no, it wasn't one with Narendra Modi, who had already talked to lots of people.

It was an interview with Rahul Gandhi who had never before spoken to a TV interviewer.

The story of how Arnab got the interview offers some insight into why he runs India's top English news channel.

Originally the interview had been promised to NDTV. An NDTV crew had even come and checked out the location. Arnab heard that NDTV was getting the interview and asked for an appointment to see Rahul Gandhi. Incredibly enough, with the NDTV interview only a couple of days away, Rahul agreed to meet Arnab.

At the meeting, Arnab laid out his pitch. Did Rahul realise how much of a lead Times Now had over the competition? Was a man who hoped to lead the Congress to victory in the election really going to give his first interview to the lowest-rated news channel in India?

When Rahul seemed startled by these questions, Arnab showed him charts and graphs that he had brought along. These illustrated the vast gap between Times Now's ratings and NDTV's.

There were counter arguments to be made. Somebody could have told Rahul that Times Now had based its success on destroying the Congress government night after night. Or, they could have argued that it did not matter what the ratings were. Any channel that had a Rahul Gandhi interview would get top ratings for that hour because everyone would watch that interview.

But nobody made those arguments. Nobody even informed NDTV that its exclusive had disappeared. Arnab seemed so convincing that Rahul agreed at once to give him the interview.

By now, everyone knows what happened in that interview. Arnab, who is always thorough, had studied the tape of one of Rahul's informal exchanges with the press and had decided how he would play it.

Somebody—we still don't know who—had clearly told Rahul that no matter what the question was, he was to repeat what the UPA had done for women's rights and for freedom of information. The interview was, eventually, almost painful to watch—like a car crash in slow motion. It finished off Rahul's campaign—at least in the eyes of educated Indians— even before it could begin.

Arnab says now that he was actually quite gentle with Rahul. He could have been much tougher. And he appreciates the politeness of the Gandhis that even after the interview was over, they asked him to stay behind for tea and sandwiches. Rahul, he says, probably knew that things had gone wrong.

But everybody else in the room kept telling him how well he had done.

It is almost an article of faith at the Times Group that no individual is allowed to keep a high profile. The executives are self-effacing. The editors shun the limelight.

All these rules were thrown to the winds when Arnab was on the ascendant. In the public mind, Times Now was run by Arnab Goswami. Even the Times brand failed to register beside Arnab's. What's more, he ran the channel as a personal crusade, ignoring the views of his proprietors and showing scant respect for such Times credos as 'news and views should never mix'.

During Arnab's glory years, Times Group insiders kept asking each other: why do the Jains allow this?

There were never any clear answers to that question except perhaps for the obvious one: because it works!

The *Times of India* is the leading English newspaper in India but under Arnab, Times Now had a lead over its rivals that vastly exceeded even the *Times of India's* lead over other papers.

This led to the other question: how can the Jains allow their channel to be built around the personality of one man? What happens if he suddenly decides to leave?

Again, the only answer possible was: oh, the Jains know he will never leave. He is very happy being number one and running his own channel. Why would he give it up, walk away from market leadership and start all over again?

Except, of course, that he did.

In November 2016, Arnab Goswami left Times Now and announced that he would start his own TV venture.

For many months, nothing happened. Other channels had believed that Arnab's absence would cripple Times Now.

Once its ratings collapsed, the race to be the new number one would begin.

But Times Now's ratings did not collapse the way that people had predicted. It continued to be a strong number one. And the fortunes of the other channels did not significantly improve.

While this jockeying for position went on, Arnab let it be known that he had joined up with Rajeev Chandrashekhar, the former telecom baron and owner of Kerala's Asianet TV network, to launch a new English channel called Republic. There would be other investors and Arnab would have a substantial stake of his own in the new venture, but nobody was very forthcoming with financial details.

Finally on 6 May 2017, Republic TV launched. Rivals were relieved when for the first couple of days it seemed as though Arnab had been in too much of a hurry to launch. The sound quality was poor. The graphic screens would not work. The switching (a technical term for shifting the picture on the screen from one camera's feed to another's feed) was slow. Only Arnab, staring mightily at a wilderness of windows, held it together.

Then, the first week's ratings came in. Not only was Republic number one, but it had more viewers than all of the English channels (including Times Now) put together.

Arnab was king once again.

The TV industry reacted with outrage. The Times Group had already sued to prevent Arnab from using his catchphrase, 'The nation wants to know'. Now it sued him for theft, claiming that one of the stories he aired was based on information he had gathered during his Times Now days and therefore belonged to the Times. According to Arnab, they even tried to file a criminal case against him in Mumbai's Azad Maidan police station.

Other channels claimed that Republic had fixed the ratings. They walked out en masse from BARC, the audience research organisation. After a week, they were persuaded to come back and told that Republic would not be allowed to commit the offences they were accusing it of. ('How does it have so many viewers in Chhattisgarh where hardly anyone watches English news?' 'How is it running on so many slots on cable networks?' That sort of thing.)

But nobody doubted one thing. Arnab was back. And he was number one.

The day I go to see Arnab at Republic TV's state-of-the-art studios in Mumbai, the National Investigation Agency (NIA) has raided Hurriyat leaders in Srinagar. Arnab has arrived at the studio at 8 a.m., and though we are due to meet at 11 a.m., he is still on the air when I arrive. His colleagues offer apologies on his behalf but are frankly admiring of his stamina. Just as he did during 26/11, Arnab has begun to virtually live in the studio during the launch period, hardly going home if he can help it.

Eventually, Arnab is done with anchoring though I get the feeling that he could well have gone on for hours more and feel slightly guilty that he has left the studio to keep our appointment.

I ask him about his legendary stamina and he attributes it to a regular life. He can get by on only three hours of sleep, he says, because he doesn't waste time on needless socialising, does not drink and does not smoke.

Obviously, his confidence has been buoyed by the remarkable success of Republic and the controversies don't seem to affect him at all. He is saddened, he says, by the Times Group's battle against him. It makes no sense, he argues, and is doomed to failure. 'They have no legal grounds and I'm shocked that they went so far as to file a police complaint. You know I have received messages from senior members of the Times team who are horrified by this kind of behaviour.'

He is unperturbed by controversies around his ratings. Republic has launched with a bang and that is all that matters. 'Ratings of over fifty per cent were never going to be sustainable in the long run,' he says philosophically. 'But I am willing to bet that out of fifty-two weeks, we will be number one for forty-eight weeks or so.'

I suggest that this sounds unduly modest. He was number one every week at Times Now, so why should Republic not top the ratings in the same way? He shrugs and suggests that forty-eight out of fifty-two won't be too bad either.

So, why did he do what everyone considered unthinkable and leave the channel the Times Group had constructed around his personality?

'I just felt that I needed to do something that was my own,' he responds.

But is Republic his own? Surely, there are other investors, apart, of course, from Rajeev Chandrashekhar?

Yes, he says, but they are content to let him run the show. He has never felt as much in control as he does now in anything he has ever done.

Was it the money? No matter how successful Times Now was, he was never going to get rich unlike, say, Prannoy Roy and Rajat Sharma who own large chunks of their channels and Rajdeep Sardesai who at the time had valuable equity in CNN-IBN?

'It is never about the money for me,' he responds. 'That has never motivated me. I don't care about being a millionaire or cashing out. I like running a channel where I am totally in control.'

We go over the usual charges. Does he mind the negative publicity? Is he annoyed that so many of his peers regard him as a joke? That he is treated as some kind of bogeyman who has destroyed the TV news business by catering to the basest instincts of his audience? What about the negative cover stories in magazines like *Caravan* and *Outlook*?

'I'll tell you what upset me,' he says. 'Vinod Mehta was one journalist I really respected and we got along. He had wanted me to release his last book but sadly, he died before that could happen.'

I tell him that I'm aware of the regard they had for each other. In Mehta's sad last years, when *Outlook's* circulation and influence were collapsing and he had been pushed out of the editorship and elevated to some meaningless post, it was Times Now that ensured that he was still relevant and visible. Night after night, Mehta would be invited to the Newshour where he would sit in his window, a glass by his side, and hold forth, expressing largely pro-UPA views that were at odds with the tone of the show.

'When Vinod died,' Arnab continues, 'I was really shaken. I wondered how *Outlook* would pay tribute to the man who created the magazine. But they put their tribute to Vinod on the back pages. And they ran a cover story attacking me. It tells you something about the kind of magazine *Outlook* had become; not that they attacked me but that they had so little regard for Vinod.'

There are other criticisms. The 'pal of the government' charge is one he is eager to refute. There is no doubt that a channel built on a platform of attacking the old elites will find something in common with a government that mobilises hatred of elites for its own political ends. But other than that, Arnab insists that he is not pro-BJP or, as some have alleged, a government cheerleader: 'We have attacked the government when we have disagreed with them, and we will do it again.'

Nor does he think that it is relevant that some of Republic's investors are pro-BJP. 'I decide the editorial policy, not them,' he says flatly.

Which takes us back to where we started. Why do so many young people think that Arnab invented news TV? Why is he the only English TV anchor who most young people below the age of twenty-five can name?

The answer is that he actually *did* invent Indian news TV. Yes, there was news TV before him but it was well-mannered and patterned on the BBC and CNN. There was no indigenous Indian TV model till Arnab came along.

In many ways, he was ahead of his time. Times Now began to put opinion at the centre of its broadcasts long before Twitter and social media made strongly-expressed opinion fashionable. He sensed that there was an anti-liberal establishment mood even before Narendra Modi made it the main plank of the BJP's appeal.

But most important, he understood how India was changing.

The first change was economic. The old middle class was being outnumbered by a newly-emerging middle class which had benefitted from a decade of growth. These were people who had no respect for (and even resented) the old ways. They had not grown up revering the BBC or even, the *Times of India*. Many had grown up in homes that took no English papers in the morning.

They were aspirational, yes. And they wanted a say in the way India was run. So they liked the idea of watching English news channels but often felt excluded from these channels by the way in which the anchors conducted the discourse.

By reaching out to the south and by treating non-English speaking guests with respect (even speaking Hindi to them if required), Arnab gave the new middle class the sense that Times Now (and now Republic) was their channel.

Arnab also recognised what demographics had done to the TV audience. All journalists keep throwing around the statistic about how sixty-five per cent of India is below twenty-one. (Or whatever the exact numbers are; they vary depending on where you read them.) But few of us realise what this means to our calling.

In effect, it means that the new TV viewer has no recollection of the bad old Doordarshan-only days. He is only dimly aware of who Prannoy Roy is.

And for the decade during which he formed his political opinions, India was run by the Congress and therefore, by implication, by the Gandhis. So, all of the ills that beset the country, from corruption to terrorism to Kashmiri separatism are associated with the Gandhis.

For many people in this age group, Narendra Modi is a figure of hope, who represents a sense that things will change for the better and that the system will become swifter, more secure and less corrupt.

Arnab probably worked out the consequences of the demographic shift before anyone else did. So, when critics accuse him of pandering to the lowest common denominator or to the politically illiterate, it doesn't bother him in the slightest.

From his perspective, he has expanded the market for English TV news, reaching out to people who would never have watched NDTV or perhaps, any English news channel at all till Times Now came along. In the week that Republic launched, the size of the total market for English news doubled as viewers left vernacular channels to watch Arnab.

Arnab is now famous. It embarrasses him. Often when he leaves the office, there are twenty or thirty people gathered near the gate to get a glimpse of him. Each time I ask about the fame factor, he brushes if off: 'It can be a nuisance,' or the more modest, 'Fortunately I live in Mumbai where there are lots of movie stars, so a TV anchor is hardly a big deal.'

So what's next? He says he has not thought beyond Republic, and expanded by launching a Hindi version of it called Republic Bharat in early 2019. But his real passion now extends beyond television. So as we wrap up the interview, he is talking enthusiastically about his digital plans. He has tied up with various non-news sites and wants to use technology to create a customised digital offering (news, entertainment, music, etc.) for anyone who subscribes. 'We will work out what appeals to you personally and we will send you content that is tailored to your interests,' he explains.

It sounds good, but it is a long way from the Newshour. But then that was a long way from Social Anthropology at Oxford.

As always, Arnab is thinking ahead.

KIRAN MAZUMDAR-SHAW

There are many misconceptions about Kiran Mazumdar-Shaw. The first of these is that she is a Bengali. Till she married John Shaw in 1998, she was only known as Kiran Mazumdar and Mazumdar is, of course, a fairly common Bengali name.

But she is not a Bengali. She is a Gujarati and the family name was probably Majmudar which was transformed to Mazumdar somewhere along the way.

The second misconception is that she started out as a research scientist: hence her latest successes at the cutting-edge of biochemistry. In fact, she started out in that most unusual of all professions for a woman of her generation—as a qualified brewmaster, that is, as somebody who knows how to brew beer.

The third misconception relates to the extent of her success. Nobody seriously disputes that she is a phenomenon, but there is always a slightly patronising edge to the praise and the phrase 'for a woman' often hovers unsaid. In fact, Mazumdar is successful by any standards—man or woman. Yes, she is India's richest self-made woman. But she is also one of India's most successful first generation entrepreneurs by any standard. Today, her wealth (shared with her husband John) stands at four billion dollars, ahead of most entrepreneurs you will hear about.

And here's the thing—almost nothing about her is typical. In most senses, she is a one-off or a true original.

Her background is unusual. Her father, Rasendra Mazumdar, may have been one of the only Gujaratis of his generation to rise to the higher echelons of the liquor business. He was the head brewmaster at Bengaluru's United Breweries and his specialisation included supervising all of that company's beer.

Kiran grew up in Bengaluru and hoped to become a doctor. When she couldn't secure admission to the medical college of her choice, she studied zoology and biology.

It was her father who suggested that perhaps she could also join the liquor business. She liked the idea because she was interested in brewing. So she went off to Australia to study malting and brewing.

In the early 1970s, when she went to Australia, the alcohol industry was largely an all-male affair everywhere in the world. Even in Australia, she was the only woman in her course. But she was good at her subject and when she graduated as a master brewer in 1975, she was top of her class.

After college, she worked for breweries and liquor-aligned companies in Australia and India but it rapidly became clear to her that in India, at least, there was little scope for growth for a woman in the liquor business.

In 1978, she accepted a job at Moray Firth Maltings in Scotland and decided that her future lay abroad. A few days before she was to leave, Kiran heard from Leslie Auchincloss, head of an Irish company called Biocon Biochemicals. Auchincloss wanted to start Indian operations which would supply enzymes to the Irish parent. Kiran deflected him by saying that she had already booked her flight to Scotland and introduced him to an existing Indian company that could meet Biocon's needs.

But Auchincloss was insistent. He was looking for an entrepreneur who could set up a business in India, he said, not for an already established company. When Kiran refused to budge, he made her an offer she could not refuse.

He wanted to talk to her new employers in Scotland and ask them to defer her appointment by a year. If at the end of twelve months of working with Biocon, Kiran still felt that she would like to join the liquor business abroad, she would be free to go. The job would still be waiting for her. And if that didn't work out, Auchincloss said, he would find another job for her abroad.

Looking back, when you consider Kiran's reluctance to become an entrepreneur, it is surprising how quickly she took to running her own company. She said yes to Auchincloss in April 1978. She then went off to Ireland for a few months to work with the parent Biocon company and returned to India in September 1978. By November she had incorporated the Indian Biocon and by the following year she was already manufacturing and exporting food manufacturing enzymes to America and Europe—the first Indian company to do so.

At the end of the first year, the business was profitable but small. She operated out of a tin shed in Bengaluru's Koramangala area, had a turnover of eight lakh rupees and a profit of one lakh. But she was already thinking big. In the 1980s, she read about a distress sale of a twenty-acre plot on the outskirts of Bengaluru. It was a long way from her little three thousand square foot operation to a twenty-acre campus, but she decided to buy the property anyway.

In 1980, Biocon acquired the plot for six lakhs. (It would prove to be a shrewd investment; Bengaluru has grown around and beyond the plot and its value has multiplied hundreds of times.)

In 1983, the new premises on Hosur Road were inaugurated and though the company was doing well, Kiran believed that Biocon India had to rise to the next level. At that time, the Japanese were masters of solid-state fermentation, a process that was far more advanced than the submerged liquid fermentation that was used in most of the world.

Kiran believed that she could get a solid-state fermentation plant built in Bengaluru. It was not easy raising the funds (ICICI eventually came in as an equity partner) and it took years to get the plant functional. But finally, Biocon did it, the first Indian firm to enter this area.

By the mid-1980s, Biocon India was a flourishing company, having grown beyond the original plan of making enzymes for the parent company in Ireland. Kiran had scoured the world for new technologies. By 1989, it was turning over two crores a year and the future looked promising.

But Auchincloss had other plans. Biocon had operations in twenty-one countries and when Unilever approached him with an offer to buy the company, he took it. Unilever paid him thirty-five million pounds sterling and took over his shares.

India remained a problem. In the 1970s when Auchincloss had set up Biocon India with Kiran, Indian laws forbade foreigners from owning more than thirty per cent of joint ventures. Auchincloss had realised that Biocon would always be a minority partner in any Indian venture; this was why he had looked for an entrepreneur who could take the other seventy per cent and drive the company.

So when the Unilever deal went through, he excluded Biocon India from the sale, arguing that as the Irish parent only owned thirty per cent, it didn't really count as a Biocon group company. But Unilever insisted on including Biocon in the deal.

And so Kiran had a new partner.

At first, Unilever did not realise the potential of Biocon India. When it did, it suddenly made every attempt to get more involved. It asked Kiran to dilute her stake and when she refused, bought out ICICI's shares. The Lever involvement helped Biocon expand but it also led to friction.

Large corporations work in mysterious ways that are hard to predict. Even while one set of Lever executives were seeking greater involvement in Biocon India's biotech initiatives, the board of Unilever decided that it had no interest in biotechnology.

In 1997, Lever sold its so-called specialty businesses (including Biocon) to the chemical gaint, ICI, for eight billion pounds sterling. Somewhere in that bundle was Biocon India, or at least Lever's shares in the company.

Kiran had anticipated that this might happen one day when she signed her agreements with Unilever (after Auchincloss had sold the Biocon group). Her deal gave her the first right of refusal in the event of a sale. In other words, Lever had to offer to sell her its Biocon shares first, before it could sell them to anyone else.

As it turned out, ICI had no particular interest in Biocon. It began to sell off many of the businesses it had acquired from Lever in bits and pieces and indicated it was quite happy to let Kiran have all of Biocon.

By then, Kiran's life had changed. In the 1990s, she had met John Shaw, who headed Madura Coats' operations in India, and after knowing each other for several years, they finally decided to get married.

It was around this time that ICI agreed to sell its shares to Kiran. The price agreed was 2.2 million dollars. One option would have been to get bank financing for the purchase.

But John and Kiran decided it would make more sense if he bought the shares himself. He had a house in London that he could sell. He sold it, bought the ICI stake and became Kiran's partner twice over, at work and at home.

Given that Biocon had always been Kiran's baby, it shouldn't have mattered that John had bought ICI out. And yet it did. Free for the first time from the stress of having to include a collaborator's intentions in her plans, she began to think even more deeply about the future. At some level, her foreign partners had always looked at Biocon India as a source of products for them and their global businesses. Now, Kiran was freed from those pressures and could think only of Biocon and what was best for the company.

Since then, Biocon has focused on areas that its foreign partners would not have been keen on, chiefly pharmaceuticals. It was believed that no Indian company could compete with the great global drug companies, but Kiran had her own approach to that. She reckoned that big pharma did not necessarily focus enough on affordable health care. Too many drugs were priced too high. So much so that people in the developing world often could not afford them.

Since the first few years of this century, Kiran has looked for ways to make medicines accessible to more people. She took Biocon into the statins sector—statins are drugs that lower cholesterol—and met with so much success that statins came to account for half of the company's revenues.

Biocon has also devoted time and money on drugs to fight diabetes. The Holy Grail in diabetes treatment is oral insulin. At present, diabetics have to inject insulin directly into the bloodstream, a situation that pleases nobody. Ideally, they should be able to just take a pill. But the perfect pill is hard to design because the insulin will first go to the stomach and only then will it enter the bloodstream, a process that is difficult to perfect.

Biocon has developed oral insulin drugs and is optimistic that it will be able to introduce them in the market in the future.

Mazumdar's other concerns seem to spring from the diseases she sees around her. She says she was traumatised watching one of her best friends dying of cancer and Biocon has concentrated on developing cancer drugs and on ways of delivering treatment that is more convenient than, say, chemotherapy. Oral cancer is largely an Indian problem. Over eighty per cent of all cases of oral cancer are found in India. Biocon is focused on treatments for it.

In her search for new drugs and new techniques, Kiran has travelled the world, often going beyond the standard borders of Big Pharma. For instance, she was surprised to discover that medical research in Cuba was cutting-edge but rarely reached the rest of the world because of Cuba's diplomatic isolation. Biocon has worked closely with Cuban institutions and researchers to develop new drugs.

Her big bets have also worked. When she pushed to develop bio-similars, there was skepticism in the market. In theory, a bio-similar should be a magic bullet. A company creates a version of a biotech drug and sells it for much less than the original drug. Given that the original drug is probably hugely overpriced (Big Pharma says that the margin is to pay for research and development), there should be a lot of scope to sell a bio-similar at a lower price.

In reality however, it hasn't always worked out that way. Getting approvals has been difficult, costs have been higher than expected and controversies have accompanied many bio-similar launches.

But now the tide seems to be turning. More and more bio-similars are getting approvals and the market seems to be taking off.

Kiran invested heavily in the development of bio-similars despite the skepticism of analysts and now that the mood has changed, there is renewed interest in Biocon which may just be sitting on a gold mine.

Some of this is reflected in Biocon's share price. Kiran took the company public in 2004 when revenues touched 500 crores (versus seventy crores when John Shaw bought out ICI) and became a billionaire soon after. Since then, her personal wealth has kept increasing and now with the renewed interest in bio-similars, oral insulin and the many other products that Biocon is developing, the stock has boomed, multiplying the Shaws' wealth.

Kiran says she is pleased that the company is doing well, but the increase in her own wealth does not affect her greatly. ('After a while, it makes no difference,' she says dismissively.) It is not the money that excites her. It is the birth of new drugs, finding new technologies and taking Indian pharmaceuticals to a level that nobody had believed they could reach.

In a sense, it is ironic that a woman who was turned down by medical college is now creating drugs that will benefit millions. But it also shows how much she learns on the job. She started the first avatar of Biocon because her brewing knowledge gave her an understanding of enzymes. But she has gone from enzymes into drugs, an area where she originally had no expertise.

It could be because she is based in Bengaluru, but I always think of her as being the next wave in a movement that was started by the IT companies in the 1990s. Like her, most of the first IT pioneers were people who came from professional middle class backgrounds and did not have business in their blood. (When Kiran's father did start his own business after retiring, it did not work.)

Like the IT pioneers, Kiran has always benchmarked Biocon to global standards and when she started out, her primary focus was the international market like, say, Infosys. Biocon is a respected company in its space all over the world. And within India, it has a reputation for never paying bribes, never dealing in black money and never cutting corners.

There was a time, at the beginning of this century, that I thought that Indian industry would follow the IT-Infosys model. Then the Satyam scam showed us that even the IT sector had its bad apples. And the next wave of billionaires tended to be people who made their money conserving scarce resources (gas, coal, spectrum, etc.) with the help of corrupt politicians.

The remarkable success of Biocon is one sign of hope. It shows us that middle class professionals can be successful entrepreneurs and that, when they run companies, they run them honestly and to global standards.

In that context, does it matter that Kiran is a woman? I guess it does for in India, the usual way for a woman to become a billionaire is to inherit the wealth from her father or husband.

Kiran Mazumdar-Shaw shows us that there is a different way. A better way.

VIJAY SHEKHAR SHARMA

By any standards, Vijay Shekhar Sharma, the founder of Paytm, is one of the great success stories of the last decade. And yet, when his name is mentioned, there is always the tiniest whiff of controversy.

Is he a self-publicist who seeks to promote himself and his company at the slightest provocation? Is he the sort of Modi bhakt who will suck up to those in power? Is this company no more than a front for the Chinese? Did he have advance notice of demonetisation—of which Paytm was a beneficiary? And should he have turned into a cheerleader for the government the very day that demonetisation was announced?

Though Vijay is reluctant to say so in so many words, you get the feeling he believes that at least some of the criticism is motivated by social resentment. There are many success stories in India but very few of today's billionaires come from backgrounds that were as poor as Vijay's. And while many of the new tycoons have put their days of poverty behind them, Vijay has never forgotten how poor he used to be and how many humiliations he suffered because of his poverty.

His father was a schoolteacher and so the family was the kind that prized education above everything else. But this also meant that they had very little money. The last salary his father drew as a teacher was Rs 23,000 a month, a sum so meagre that even now, Vijay is shocked by how little schoolteachers are paid. 'We expect them to create a new India, and then we pay our teachers nothing,' he says with more than a trace of bitterness.

They were so poor, he says, that till he finished college, they could not afford a TV set. They couldn't even afford to buy clothes for the kids. Vijay's wardrobe was so basic that if he had to go to a wedding, he was made to wear his school uniform because those were the only nice clothes he had.

It got so bad that even his cousins refused to play with him because Vijay and his family were poor relatives, people they regarded as being nothing.

Vijay told me this story in a TV interview. Usually when people are before the cameras, they take care to show their best face. Not Vijay. Pretty much every mention of his childhood caused him to burst into tears.

Even relatively innocuous bits of conversation took him back to his poverty-stricken childhood. He talked about asking Nandan Nilekani to serve on the Paytm board. Nandan refused, arguing reasonably enough that this could constitute a conflict of interest with his other responsibilities.

This was enough to get the tears rolling again. 'You are the first person I have met, after my father, who cares about conflict of interest,' Vijay told Nandan between sobs. When he retold this story on TV, recalling how his father had stopped taking private tuitions when he became principal of the school where he worked because of potential conflicts of interest, Vijay wept loudly again.

But there were learnings too from that very deprived upbringing. Vijay recalls that old saying, 'Character is what you are in the dark.' His father taught him, he says, that even if you are a person of no consequence and not noticed by anyone, you had to remain true to your values.

It was a lesson that served him well. When he came to Delhi from Aligarh, he was, he says, 'a total nobody'. On an occasion in Delhi, he had a choice between walking for hours or taking a bus. He chose to walk, and saved the Rs 10 fare because he thought he could get something to eat with that money.

'I was nothing, a nobody. I had nothing to lose. I could have done what I wanted. Who would have known?' he says. 'But because my father had taught me that you must stick to your values even when nobody is looking, I stayed on the right path.'

One interesting consequence of his poverty-stricken childhood was that he became obsessively patriotic. 'I had no TV, no money, nothing, so I concentrated on our nation. I grew to really love India and to always want to serve it. Even now, if I attend a flag hoisting, I burst into tears. If I hear a patriotic song, I cry. The national anthem always makes me cry. I have been at formal functions and when they play the national anthem, I find myself crying while the people around me ask what is wrong.'

When Vijay came to Delhi, his English was poor—he was after all, the first member of his family to speak the language. It put him at a disadvantage but fortunately Hindi media came to his aid. He worked with the India Today group, owners of the TV channel Aaj Tak, and began finally to feel at home in the big city.

Then, like many people who are not confident of their language skills, he found a saviour in digital technology. 'I had two mission statements for myself,' he remembers. 'No greed. No entitlement.' He then started his own internet company with telecom operators as his customers. But because he had no capital, he had to borrow the eight lakhs required to start the venture. He found the money but at a usurious twenty-four per cent rate of interest.

The company did well, and on paper it was profitable. But because the telecom operators would not pay their bills on time, he had a serious cash flow problem and could not pay the interest on the loan. Eventually he sold half the company just to pay back the loan.

However, Vijay's business began to grow and he came to be regarded as a bright young man to watch in the technology business. Except, of course, that Vijay was no technology expert. He hadn't got into IIT (his lack of fluency in English may have been the problem) and his tech skills were not great.

So why technology? He is defensive. 'How does it matter?' he asks. 'Did Elon Musk know anything about automobiles before he entered the sector? Does he know anything about space? That hasn't stopped him from entering the sectors.'

This may be true, but it is not an answer to the question. What is more likely is that, like many other middle-class kids of his generation, Vijay found that technology allowed him to bypass the hierarchies of old. Technology empowered the young. They did not have to come from business families. It did not matter how good their English was. In many ways, technology created a level playing field.

Besides, as Vijay says, 'It often helps to be an outsider. People with expertise try and think along the same lines. It is outsiders who understand how things can be done differently.'

The rest of the story is reasonably well known. Paytm which allowed people to transfer money via smartphones became the perfect product for its times. It was egalitarian because almost everyone in urban India now is a mobile phone user (according to one estimate, there are more households with mobile phones in India than households with toilets).

Vijay became pals with Jack Ma, the Chinese tech billionaire who is one of the world's richest people. Ma's company Alibaba invested in Paytm and more recently, Warren Buffett, the legendary investor bought into Paytm. When I spoke to Vijay, he was India's youngest billionaire with a net worth in excess of two billion US dollars. Now, after the Buffett deal, he is probably worth even more.

But the money has done little to change Vijay. He does not encash his shares and continues to live relatively simply. He does not own a house and lives in rented accommodation. Friends say that he doesn't even spend his money on buying his wife a gift. I asked him about it and his response was: 'My wife does not want expensive gifts.'

So what does it mean to him to be a billionaire?

'Money is only an opportunity,' he says. 'History does not remember rich people. It only remembers people who contributed something or changed the way we lived.'

Vijay's contribution to the way we live, he thinks, will be the banking revolution. He has already changed the way in which payments are made. Now, with his Paytm Bank, he thinks that he will be able to provide a superior kind of banking in India. 'People using our bank will know that their assets are safe. There will be no risky lending. No bad debts. We will charge lower service fees.'

Vijay looks at Uber, Ola, the airline reservation apps and all the ground-breaking uses that the internet has been put to. 'All of these apps have changed the way in which we do things forever. The Paytm Bank will do exactly that for banking. People will never bank in the same way again.'

Inevitably, he adds, 'I want to be known as the man who revolutionised banking in India. And on my gravestone I want it to say, "O Great Creator".'

Beneath the bombast though, are some perceptive observations about how technology has changed the nature of Indian business. The first wave of tech success stories were creators of what Vijay calls 'India as the backroom.' Their clients were abroad and they offered tech services to the world. Most (if not all) made the bulk of their money by offering services to businesses, not consumers.

Vijay's generation however has changed the rules of the game. They have been assisted by the decades of growth in India. Earlier, there was no market in India because most people did not use computers. But the rise of smartphones and the new prosperity have changed all that. Now, most Indians use some form of technology.

So Paytm and the other second-generation companies now have a readymade market of the sort that was not available to the first lot of tech companies. This allows them to engage directly with consumers in the domestic market—a phenomenon that gives them unprecedented access to one of the world's largest populations.

Most of this is a creation of circumstances and not some tribute to the ingenuity of this generation of tech entrepreneurs, but Vijay thinks it is a triumph nevertheless. 'In the old days,' he says, 'India used to be the back-office of the world. Now India is the market and people from all over the world are working for us as we do our best to offer services to Indians.'

The rhetoric is not atypical. Nearly everything Vijay says or does has a strong patriotic, nationalistic slant. He says he can't help it. That is just the way he is; the sort of guy who tears up when they play *Jana Gana Mana*.

Fair enough. But it does make him something of an oddity in the global tech community where the philosophy is that the purpose of technology is to cut across borders, not celebrate national identity. Steve Jobs did not salute the Stars and Stripes regularly. The founders of, say, Uber and Google, do not treat their triumph as nationalistic American achievements.

Besides, say his critics, all this flag-waving stuff is a bit rich because Paytm is essentially a Chinese company, majority-owned by Jack Ma's Alibaba. And if you want to play the patriotic card, then China may not be the perfect partner.

I asked Vijay about this and more specifically about the criticism of Paytm from a banker-turned-politician, who is now deceased. Vijay was not pleased. He refused to respond, saying that the lady in question was a politician. But his broad answer to the question was that while Paytm had substantial Chinese investment, the Paytm Bank was an Indian entity mostly owned, created and managed by Indians.

Then there are the controversies relating to Vijay's admiration of Narendra Modi, in particular the demonetisation furore. Modi announced demonetisation at around 9 p.m. one night. The next morning, major newspapers carried a full page cover ad from Paytm hailing both Modi and demonetisation.

The timing struck people as odd. Major newspapers in Delhi are ready to go to press by around 10:30 or 11:00 p.m. How had Paytm managed to get an ad ready in such record time? More to the point, how had the company managed to get it into the papers?

A full page cover ad requires newspapers to change their entire pagination or—at the very least—pull out an ad that had already been accepted.

As unlikely as it sounded, the suspicion grew that perhaps Paytm or Vijay himself had been tipped off about demonetisation. How else could the ad have appeared in the next day's paper?

Vijay says he found out about demonetisation at the same time as everyone else. His teams got the ad ready in record time and the newspapers delayed their closing times to accommodate the ad. This claim is met with eye-rolling skepticism by Vijay's critics but knowing how cash-strapped newspapers will cheerfully push back their printing schedule for ads, I believe him.

But since then, Vijay has routinely attracted criticism. He welcomed demonetisation with such glee and praised Modi with such enthusiasm that many joked that Vijay was treating the entire demonetisation exercise (which caused pain and suffering to many) as no more than a marketing exercise organised by Modi to help his business.

A year later when he donated ten thousand rupees to help those affected by the Kerala floods and tweeted to explain how Paytm could be used to make donations, he walked into another storm. Was this a charitable donation or a publicity stunt for Paytm? And considering that he was worth billions, should Vijay be donating only ten thousand rupees?

I am guessing that Vijay has learned to live with the criticism. When you draw his attention to this, he responds with lofty rhetoric about how anyone who has tried to do something different has faced criticism, etc., etc.

I am on Vijay's side, though. Yes, he can be brash. But that's okay. He has the right to be that. What's more important is that he has come out of nowhere to take on the old, sloppy ways in which people conducted financial transactions. And he has transformed the entire scenario.

Even without the nationalism and the billions of dollars he has made, that is a considerable achievement.

GAGGAN ANAND

It was one of those coincidences that only seem significant years later. In early 2011, I was walking down Soi Langsuan, a Bangkok street that was noted (in that era) for the quality of its restaurants and live music venues.

I was intrigued by a sign that read 'Gaggan Progressive Indian Cuisine'. Progressive? I had heard of 'progressive' as a term for Left-leaning political activists. And in the 1970s, it was the term used by rock musicians who took themselves very seriously (Pink Floyd, Jethro Tull, etc.) to categorise their music, lest they got mistaken for mere pop stars.

But 'Progressive Cuisine?' That was a new one.

Intrigued, I walked into the house where the restaurant was situated, a few metres from the main road. The man at the reception desk was Thai and told me, with typical Thai politeness that he was sorry but the restaurant was full.

I was a little surprised. Indian restaurants are rarely full in Bangkok. And besides, this was clearly a new establishment. I knew Soi Langsuan well and I had never seen this before.

As I turned around to leave, an Indian man came rushing out. 'I am the chef,' he said, a little breathlessly. 'It will take half an hour but we will find a table for you. Can you come back?' Now I was even more intrigued.

Fine, I said, I'll go and have a drink somewhere and come back. When I did return, my table was ready. The chef now introduced himself. His name was Gaggan Anand, he said. We had met, first at the Taj in Delhi and then, more recently, at the Lebua Hotel in Bangkok. Frankly, I had no recollection of either meeting but I was struck by his passion so I said that I would eat whatever he recommended. 'Leave it to me,' he said.

It was a wise decision because Gaggan served me some of the most unusual Indian food I had eaten. There was a sphere of yoghurt which melted in your mouth to release the flavours of papri chaat. Later, he served a deconstructed butter chicken, along with many other intriguing courses, and for dessert there was a vanilla ice-cream into which he had infused the flavour of cigar smoke.

The ice-cream was a homage, he said, to one of his idols, the American chef Thomas Keller. He had never eaten Keller's food but had followed his career.

But what about the other stuff? I asked. Where had those dishes come from? Well, he said, he had spent two months at the Alicia Foundation in Spain, learning the techniques of molecular gastronomy from Ferran Adria's collaborators. At the time, Adria's El Bulli was the number one restaurant in the world and Ferran was the most influential chef of the twenty-first century. (He probably still is.)

I knew a little about molecular gastronomy (though I never ate at El Bulli) so I recognised some of the inspirations. One of El Bulli's signature dishes was the 'olive'. It looked like an olive but when you put it in your mouth, it melted, giving out the most intense olive flavour imaginable. Obviously Gaggan had learnt the molecular techniques in Spain and used them to create his papri chaat sphere.

There were Indian chefs who were fooling around with molecular techniques (usually, quite ineptly) but I had never before come across somebody who applied the techniques to Indian food, inventing new dishes of his own.

I was impressed and wrote about Gaggan in *Rude Food*, my column for the *Hindustan Times*. At around the same time, the food writer John Krich featured the restaurant in the Asian edition of *Time* magazine. And a buzz grew around the restaurant and Gaggan's fresh take on Indian food.

But I never expected—and nor I think, did Gaggan— what would happen next. The controversial but immensely influential list of the World's Top 50 restaurants found place for Gaggan. Then the same organisation started an Asia list. Gaggan first made the top ten and then zoomed to number one, a position he has held for an unprecedented four years in a row.

Netflix included Gaggan in its prestigious *Chef's Table* series, alongside the world's greatest chefs, introducing his food to a new audience. International food writers raved about Gaggan's culinary wizardry. The restaurant, already quite successful (remember, they were full the night I walked in), became a phenomenon: you needed to book several months in advance to get a table.

And Gaggan is now one of the hottest chefs in the world. He has gone far, far beyond anything any Indian chef has ever achieved.

Who would have thought it when I first walked through that door on Soi Langsuan?

Gaggan Anand is not your obvious candidate for international fame. A Punjabi, he grew up in Kolkata as an only child in a home where there was never enough money. His father ran a series of small businesses, all of which failed, and the family struggled to make ends meet. Because they were English-speaking and well-educated, theirs was a genteel kind of poverty. They had the manners required to become part of the middle class but lacked the cash required to keep up appearances.

Gaggan grew up, by his own admission, as a slightly wild child, with a passion for rock music. His favourites were the so-called 'progressive' bands (so that's where he gets it from!) and he became the drummer in the college rock group.

But cooking was in the genes. His father was a good cook and his mother's traditional Punjabi food was so good that when the family ran out of money (which was often), she would cook curries and snacks and sell them to people who wanted to throw parties at home.

Early on, he decided that he would not continue with college but would follow in his mother's footsteps and try and make a living out of cooking. Some of his relatives were incredulous but his mother knew it was the right decision: Gaggan was at his best when he worked with his hands.

He got into hotel school and chose to go to faraway Thiruvananthapuram, a city he had never been to before. Unlike many other students who dreamt of becoming general managers of hotels, Gaggan was sure that he wanted to cook. He recalls that he quickly became one of the best students in class, though his contemporaries remember him slightly differently. 'Mad fellow. Used to get drunk and start playing the drums on the table or wherever he was,' one of them told me. And that also sounds like Gaggan.

When he finished his course, he joined the Taj group of hotels where he had mixed experiences. He admired senior chefs like Arvind Saraswat who had given their lives to the craft and was pleased to work with middle level chefs like

Pradeep Sharma. Pradeep had just finished working with Richard Neat, a two Michelin star chef from London who briefly ran an haute cuisine restaurant at the Delhi Taj.

Gaggan watched, fascinated, as Pradeep taught him how to make Neat's classic dishes 'I still remember them,' he said. 'There was a mille-feuille of foie gras which gave me some experience of the best way to cook foie gras. And then there was a duck breast rolled in a rosti potato cover with a sauce of lentils cooked with bacon. This was my first experience of cuisine of this quality and I found it fascinating.'

But Gaggan was not entirely at home in the Taj kitchen. He thought that the staff was organised a little like the army, with clear distinctions between officers and enlisted men. 'The cooks who did the actual cooking, who had maybe twenty years' experience, earned less than half of what we, as young catering college graduates, were paid. It made no sense to me.'

And when he worked in the kitchens of the Taj Palace, he felt he was out in the jungle: 'This was a huge banquet hotel with many chefs and the atmosphere was really unpleasant with too much negative energy. Your own contemporaries would try and destroy you. One of them, who I will not name because he is quite well known today, really dug the knife into my back.'

There was a personal component too. From his teens onwards, Gaggan had been in love with a Bengali girl. When he began working at the Taj, she moved to Delhi to be with him and they began secretly living together. Inevitably her parents found out and insisted that they get married. So, much earlier than he should have, and way before his career could stabilise, Gaggan Anand found himself married. (A quick registration ceremony at Delhi's Tis Hazari court was all it took.)

Almost from the start, the relationship was stormy. Gaggan says his wife was overly possessive but, from all accounts, he was not the most tranquil person either during this phase. When the dual pressures of the dog-eat-dog Taj Palace kitchen and the tension at home got too much, he began missing work or going in late. His colleagues complained to the top chefs in the hope that Gaggan would be sacked.

Finally, says Gaggan, he decided that he could not take it any longer. One day, he drove his motorcycle to the roundabout that led to the Taj Palace, reached a sudden decision and turned around and drove off.

He never went back to the Taj Palace.

Now that he was jobless, Gaggan and his wife went back to Kolkata. His intention was to set up a catering business but this was less easy than it sounded. With his Taj training and his own passion for quality, he refused to cut corners, only turning out food that he could be proud of. But as the economic pressures mounted, he took whatever work he could get. He started churning out meals in bulk at low cost and took contracts to supply entire offices and even the staff at a famous pizza outlet (who, presumably, had the good sense not to eat the pizzas they were selling to paying customers).

Gaggan says he worked eighteen- to nineteen-hour days, involved his wife in the business and then watched what had begun as a small venture born out of desperation become a super success.

But his marriage remained rocky and after one dispute over how to handle a client, he handed over the business to his wife and began looking for consultancies elsewhere. (He found them, setting up restaurants for clients in Nagaland and other places.) The marriage, though severely dysfunctional, survived, and his wife and he continued to live in the same house.

The tipping point came when one of the people Gaggan had consulted for called him about a new Indian restaurant in Bangkok. It was going to be a big budget venture so could Gaggan find them a chef?

Something clicked inside Gaggan's head when he heard about Bangkok. 'Forget about looking for a chef,' he said on impulse. 'I'll do it myself.'

Today, Gaggan remembers, 'My wife was standing next to me and when she heard me saying that I would go to Bangkok, she actually hit me.'

But he went anyway.

Gaggan hadn't really been abroad till he got to Bangkok. And he loved it on sight. He liked being alone. He liked the energy of the Thai capital. And he was excited by the idea of opening a proper Indian restaurant again.

The new restaurant was called Red and Gaggan intended it to be more modern and more stylish than most of the ageing competition in the Indian restaurant sector in Thailand. It had no one owner but multiple partners, a source of strife in the future.

But at first everything went well. The restaurant opened to good reviews, Gaggan made a reasonable living and the city's Indians took Red to their hearts. Among Gaggan's regular guests was Deepak Ohri, then Bangkok's hottest restaurateur after the spectacular success of the rooftop Sirocco. Another less high profile guest was Rajesh Kewalramani, an executive with DTAC, the Thai telecom giant. Both men would go on to play important roles in Gaggan's life.

Once the restaurant was firmly established, Gaggan's problems with the owners began. On one occasion he was accused of wiping sweat from his brow in the kitchen in such a manner that it could have fallen into the curry he was cooking. At first Gaggan was mystified by the accusation but then he discovered that the owners had put a spycam in the kitchen to keep a watch on him.

He lost his temper, took some atta (wheat flour dough) and placed it over the lens of the camera, obscuring its vision. Then he took chilli powder and made a line at the edge of the kitchen. 'This is the Lakshman rekha,' he declared dramatically. 'No one except for a chef will cross it.'

But once relations between an employee and his bosses have soured beyond repair, it is hard for things to ever get back to normal. Gaggan's wife had flown out to join him in Bangkok (the catering business in Kolkata now having failed) and the dysfunctional relationship added to his tensions.

Finally, as the pressure mounted, he broke up messily with his wife who flew back to Kolkata.

Gaggan's exit from Red was triggered by a tiny incident. He gave a free drink to a guest and was accused of exceeding his authority. He said it was the chef's prerogative. The owners did not agree.

He says now that he does not remember the exact chain of events that led to his exit but he recalls being asked to sit on a chair while the owners and managers surrounded him, pointing fingers and hurling accusations. He was so overwrought that he cried uncontrollably.

That phase of his life was also over.

Unemployed in a strange land, Gaggan picked up the phone and called Deepak Ohri. He remembered that Ohri had told him if he ever wanted to leave Red, there would be a job for him at Lebua, the hotel where Sirocco was located. Now he asked Ohri for that job.

By then, Deepak Ohri was a phenomenon in Bangkok. Using the success of Sirocco as a springboard, he had turned

Lebua, the hotel it was located in, into a gourmet destination. Breeze, an open-air Oriental restaurant, was doing well and Mezzaluna, an Italian restaurant run by two chefs called the Suhrings who were identical twins, served some of the best European food in Bangkok.

The gap in the offering was an Indian restaurant and Ohri hoped to turn Lebua's underused coffee shop into a trendy Indian place called Cafe Mozu. Gaggan was tasked with making that happen.

'Deepak Ohri saved me,' Gaggan says now. 'Not only did he give me a job but when the people at Red sued me, he handled the lawsuit and made it go away. I am not sure I could have continued staying in Bangkok if he was not around at that time.'

Gaggan imported two cooks from India but as food trials for the new restaurant progressed, it soon became clear to him that Lebua was not really interested in a modern Indian restaurant. The management wanted more traditional Indian food and while Gaggan was capable of turning that out, the idea did not excite him.

Rajesh Kewalramani, another of his regulars from Red, had kept in touch and one day, Gaggan called him and said that he was tired of opening restaurants for others and wanted to do something for himself. Why didn't Kewalramani partner with him in a new venture?

Kewalramani was a salaried employee of a telecom company (a job he still retains) and did not have the capital required to start a restaurant. Fortunately, his brother was a successful businessman and willing to invest. He found another partner in a local Indian businessman and told Gaggan that he would take a loan from his bank so that he could match the money being put up by the others.

Once the partnership was in place (by around 2008), Gaggan and Rajesh confronted their real problem: what kind of restaurant did they want to open?

Gaggan said he wanted to do modern Indian food. But he didn't want to simply tinker around with the plating as many chefs before him had done. He wanted to go deep into new dishes and play around with familiar flavours.

Kewalramani remembers asking Gaggan: 'What is your real passion? What is it that you would do if anything and everything seemed possible?'

Gaggan told him that he was fascinated by the work that Ferran Adria had done in the field of molecular gastronomy and he would love to work at El Bulli.

There was a problem with that. El Bulli did not accept stagiers, the culinary world's equivalent of poorly paid (or entirely unpaid) interns. A stage meant that you worked at the lowest rung of the ladder. You saw how the dishes were made, but you were not necessarily part of the action.

A more attractive option was the Alicia Foundation, set up by Adria and El Bulli, which looked at the technology and techniques that went into the creation of El Bulli's cuisine. This was not a restaurant. It was a scholarly enterprise but it had the advantage of allowing Gaggan to understand the philosophy behind the food and to master the techniques without worrying too much about the current menu at El Bulli.

Except that this was also impossible to get into.

Gaggan and Rajesh found a phone number and kept calling it. On their twentieth attempt, somebody answered. Gaggan explained who he was and why he wanted to study at the foundation. The woman at the other end of the line was friendly but said she was unable to help because too many

people wanted to come to the foundation. Even if they found
a way to fit Gaggan in, it would take several months.

No, said Gaggan, I need to come soon because I want to
open my own restaurant quickly.

Eventually, the foundation gave in and asked Gaggan to
come right away. Gaggan thinks, looking back, that this was
because they had never had an Indian chef apply to join them
before. Perhaps they were getting tired of all the Americans
and Europeans and were intrigued by the idea of an Indian
who wanted to study the technology.

Rajesh and the partners kept their word. They had asked
Gaggan to tell them what he really wanted to do. And now
that it was possible, they would pay for Gaggan to go.

From Gaggan's perspective, the two months he spent at
the foundation significantly altered his perspective on food.
He had learned Indian and European techniques during his
time with the Taj. But now a whole new world opened up.
He could make his food crisp without deep-frying it. He
could use water-baths to tenderise fish without losing any of
its flavour. He could play around with the shapes and forms
of ingredients.

It is important to remember that while he would often cook
for everyone at the foundation and that he met Ferran Adria,
Gaggan did not actually work at El Bulli. So unlike many of
the chefs who have worked in that kitchen, he did not simply
want to reproduce what he had seen there. Instead, because he
made friends with the people who created the techniques, he
went far deeper into the philosophy behind El Bulli.

Two months later, when Gaggan returned to Bangkok,
Rajesh and he began searching for a location for the restaurant.
His parting from Lebua had not been without its share of
acrimony (basically they felt that he owed it to them to stay),

so he needed to find a new gig quickly. But even as Rajesh and he settled on an old house in Soi Langsuan as the location, civil unrest erupted and Bangkok more or less shut down. So work on the restaurant came to a standstill and the partners waited for things to return to normal.

Gaggan used that time to create his menu. By then, everybody knew about the El Bulli olive but he felt that the technique would work better with yoghurt. Except that yoghurt already had calcium from the milk so he needed to reduce the calcium in the solution that Adria used to make his spheres. His training at the foundation began to pay off as he used his understanding of the new techniques to create his own kind of Indian food.

Finally, in late 2010, the restaurant opened, with its now notorious claim to serve 'progressive' food. The first customers were mainly Thai, which is unusual because Thais don't normally frequent Indian restaurants. Then European expatriates became regulars. And only at the very end did Indians venture in to try the food.

By the end of the first month, the partners knew that they had a winner on their hands. They reckoned that they could recover their entire investment in a couple of years (which they did). But what they had not reckoned on was the global praise that would be showered on Gaggan.

From the very start, there was always the danger that cynics might see Gaggan's food as gimmicky. After all, molecular gastronomy had been brought into disrepute by chefs who used it solely to play tricks on customers. But what the partners had not realised was how ready Indian cuisine was for the odd gimmick or two.

For much too long, Indian food abroad had been dull and heavy, with greasy brown sauces and mounds of yellow rice.

Gaggan brought the joy back into the cuisine. Not only was his food light (he cut down on the carb content), but it was also witty. At no stage, however, did he compromise on the flavours—his experience as an Indian chef came in handy—so if he made a butter chicken gravy, it would taste like the real thing, no matter how much he played around with the form or deconstructed it. His own ebullience, the 'progressive' rock he played at the restaurant and the jokiness of the menu turned eating at Gaggan into a joyful experience. Suddenly there was laughter, music and joy in the food—rare qualities at Indian restaurants abroad.

At what stage did Gaggan cease to be among the world's best Indian chefs and become simply one of the world's great chefs?

It is hard to say, but once the acclaim started pouring in and the restaurant was more profitable than anyone had ever imagined, Gaggan's attitude to his food changed. He became less interested in crowd pleasers like his spherified papri chaat and stopped worrying about how customers would react to each dish. He threw away the a'la carte menu and declared that he would only serve one menu for the whole restaurant. (Well, not exactly, because vegetarians still get their own menu.) If people didn't like it, well that was tough.

For many chefs, the decision to offer customers no choice and to throw out some of the best-selling items on the menu could have spelled commercial suicide. But my sense is that it was only after he made that gutsy decision that Gaggan really came into his own as a chef. He moved away from the molecular tricks—he still uses the techniques but he does it so cleverly that guests may not notice. He allowed his set menu to wander around the world in the middle of the meal before bringing it back to Indian flavours for the last courses.

And he treated nothing as settled or sacred. For instance, one of his signature dishes (now much copied) is called Charcoal. This consists of a hard, black shell (the charcoal of the name) encasing a chop of delicately spiced fish. At first guests could not work out that the filling was fish though he had intended the dish to be a homage to the Bengali fish chops of his Calcutta days.

But ever since the dish became famous, Gaggan has abandoned the fish filling and experimented with new ingredients. During my last visit to his restaurant, I had the fourth version of Charcoal. I could not guess what the filling was and neither could anyone else at my table. It turned out to be white asparagus.

In the old days, he would have worried about tinkering with a dish that people still fly in from all over the world to try.

Now he doesn't care.

That's the kind of courage and passion that has elevated him to becoming one of the world's great chefs.

One other factor has been crucial in Gaggan's development as a chef. He first went to Japan on holiday with his Thai wife, Pui. They did not have much money to begin with when they planned the trip, but by the time they were ready to leave, the restaurant had taken off. Gaggan duly upgraded their air tickets to business class, brought an expensive camera and decided to hit the top restaurants of Japan.

Except that it is not easy to get into the best Japanese restaurants, no matter how much money you have. Many are small (fifteen seats or so) places that only allow regulars—more like private clubs than restaurants. Fortunately Gaggan met some extremely well-connected Japanese well-wishers who took him to the best restaurants in Tokyo.

Japan may have been more influential than Spain when it came to Gaggan's style of cooking. It was in Japan that he first learnt how important it was to treat ingredients with respect. He discovered how the taste of a fish changes depending on how you cut it. He learned that when it came to sashimi, fresh was not always the best. A great sushi-sashimi chef will refrigerate a piece of tuna till the enzymes inside it have maximised the flavour. He found out that a scallop from Hokkaido could differ substantially from one a few hundred miles away. He was introduced to the complex world of Japanese tea. He was taught how to find umami—the prized fifth taste that is integral to Japanese cooking—in tea.

It was the beginning of a love affair that has still to run its course. Now Gaggan goes to Japan every two months or so. He has found a kindred spirit in a Japanese chef called Takeshi Fukuyama aka Goh, and the two of them cook together regularly, combining flavours and creating new dishes out of their combined experiences.

The Japanese influence is evident in Gaggan's food but it is even more apparent in the other things he does. At Meatilicious, the steakhouse that his wife runs, they serve high quality Japanese beef at prices that are far lower than anywhere else in Bangkok. Gaggan studied the marbling of beef (the key component in Japanese wagyu) and found a cow farmer whose beef he liked. He bought in bulk directly from the farmer, cutting out the middlemen, and now he can sell some of the best Japanese beef at prices that make it accessible to more people.

He has also opened a new restaurant in collaboration with a Japanese tofu maker. Like most Indians, Gaggan was agnostic about tofu when he first came to Thailand, but the repeated visits to Japan have turned him into a true believer. He says that he never realised how delicious tofu could be and the new restaurant will introduce Thais to tofu of a calibre they have never encountered before.

In 2017, as Gaggan became Asia's best restaurant for the third year in a row, the press was filled with stories about how the restaurant would close. Gaggan had had enough, the papers and blogs reported, he was ready to call it a day.

As all this talk was at its height, I flew to Bangkok to talk to Gaggan for this book. We decided that we would get no peace at his restaurant and resolved to meet elsewhere. He chose afternoon tea at the historic Authors' Lounge at the Oriental Hotel where, of course, he was recognised by the Thai serving staff.

I began by asking whether he was serious about closing the restaurant. Yes, he was, he said. But the press had jumped the gun. He would keep it going till 2020 before walking away from it.

What would he do then?

Well, his wife and he planned to spend much of their time in Japan and he would cook with chef Goh. Perhaps they would open a small, experimental restaurant in a remote part of Japan.

Would Gaggan close down?

Yes and no. The restaurant would keep going. But he wouldn't cook there. He hoped that one of his sous chefs, possibly Rydo, the Indonesian who runs the kitchen when Gaggan is travelling, would take over.

Would it still be called Gaggan?

No. It would not.

Why was he doing it? Was he scared of failure? Nobody lasts at number one for very long. Was he just jumping before he was pushed?

He thought he had at least another few years in the top five, he said, without false modesty. The food at Gaggan had got better and he believed that any fair-minded critic would see that.

Why, then, was he walking away from Gaggan?

Well, because he did not want to spend the rest of his life doing the same thing. He enjoyed what he did at Gaggan but he enjoyed it because he knew he would not keep doing it for the rest of his life. It was still a passion. He wanted to get out and do something different before it became an obligation.

So will he do it? Will he walk away from Gaggan?

I believe he will.

Nearly everything he has done over the last year hints at an exit strategy. He now has a restaurant empire that no longer depends on his own culinary talents. When the Suhring twins from Mezzaluna at Lebua wanted to set up on their own, Gaggan and Rajesh put up half the investment. So Gaggan's empire now has a Suhring, Meatlicious and Gaa, right opposite his original restaurant, run by the former Noma chef Garima Arora. There will be a wine bar in the Gaggan complex. Then the tofu restaurant should launch soon. And he is still toying with the idea of a curry house.

'These are my savings.' he says. They will provide him with enough of a living to never have to work for money ever again. His wife and he have bought a duplex apartment in the tony Sathorn area, so that's another investment that can only appreciate.

'At the moment, I have gold in my hand,' he says. 'Everything I touch makes money for me. This is the time to make my retirement plans.'

And when those plans have been put into action, what then?

Well, there will be two Gaggan Anands: the successful restaurateur and the wild and crazy chef who travels the world and cooks only for fun.

But this is Gaggan we are talking about. So even the cooking for fun will yield truly great dishes! Great chefs never retire. They just cook up something new.

(Since I wrote this profile, Gaggan fell out with his original investors, and resigned from the restaurant which then closed. His staff walked out with him and they opened a new restaurant called Gaggan Anand which should be flourishing by the time you read this.)

SHASHI THAROOR

Here's the funny thing about Shashi Tharoor. If he had not been a former Union minister and a three-term Member of Parliament or the most successful Indian in the history of the United Nations, he would still have been famous. Except that he would have been famous for a reason that hardly gets a mention these days.

Tharoor is one of India's biggest-selling authors. One of his recent books influenced an entire generation of Indians who now quote Tharoor's arguments in debates. And for many liberals, he is something of a poster boy. Not only does he write books on subjects that liberals hold dear—the legacy of Jawaharlal Nehru, the perversion of Hinduism by the Right-wing, etc.—but, at a time when secular liberalism is in decline all over India, Tharoor turns these subjects into bestsellers.

In a way this is appropriate because Tharoor first made his name as a writer. As a small boy, he had indifferent health and often stayed in bed for long stretches. Books were his only friends during that phase and he read Enid Blyton as well as adventure stories by the likes of Capt. W.E. Johns, creator of the Biggles series about a fighter pilot.

These books influenced his first formal attempt at writing: a short action-packed novella, published in instalments when

Shashi was around thirteen years old in the *Junior Statesman* (now defunct), a leading youth magazine of its era. (Which oddly enough, is how I—and thousands of other young readers like me—first heard of him.)

Tharoor continued writing (amongst others for *Sunday* and the *Telegraph*) throughout his childhood in Calcutta and then began writing for Delhi papers when he went to St. Stephen's College at Delhi University. Although his articles were much admired, he had no great desire to be a full-time writer. He went off instead to America for a post-graduate course.

By the time he joined the UN, Tharoor was ready to write again. But he chose fiction (perhaps his day job limited what he could say). His first book, a re-imagining of the Mahabharata, called *The Great Indian Novel* was published in 1989 to good reviews in India and the US. Three years later, *Show Business,* his second novel (about an Amitabh Bachchan-like actor) found commercial and literary success in India.

Two more works of fiction followed, *The Five Dollar Smile*, a collection of short stories, and *Riot*, a novel inspired by the accounts he had heard from a civil servant friend whom he had known at St. Stephen's (the friend, Harsh Mander, then went on to publish a non-fiction account of the same riot).

By the end of his UN stint, Shashi Tharoor was more successful than any Indian had ever been at that organisation. He worked closely with Kofi Annan (when he was Secretary General), headed the UN's biggest department and went on to stand for Secretary General himself, with the backing of the Indian government (his candidacy seemed very promising till the US threw its weight behind Ban Ki-Moon).

Though Tharoor had made his name as a well-regarded writer of fiction, he was at a disadvantage because of his UN profile. Other writers thought of him as somebody who only wrote in his spare time (true enough, but hardly a reflection on the quality of his work) and therefore, not a full-time writer at all. And while the reviews were always good (from such publications as the *New York Times*) nothing he wrote was regarded as Booker Prize material.

All that changed when he wrote his first significant work of non-fiction. In 1996, David Davidar, Tharoor's editor at Penguin India, called him to ask if he would write something for the fiftieth anniversary of India's Independence? Tharoor agreed and wrote *India: From Midnight to the Millennium and Beyond*, a serious but endearing account of India's journey, mixing history with his own memories.

It was a book that was expected to do well anyway but it received an unexpected boost because of Bill Clinton, then President of the United States. Clinton was on holiday in Martha's Vineyard. On one occasion, he went into a bookshop and bought two books. One of them, the US press reported, was *India: From Midnight to the Millennium and Beyond*.

Just as John F. Kennedy's remark—that he was reading a book by Ian Fleming (one of his favourite authors)—had led to James Bond's success in the US, so Clinton's purchase of Tharoor's book suddenly made Americans curious about the author. It soon became obvious that Clinton had enjoyed reading the book. He met Tharoor at a dinner and spoke incessantly about the book and the success of the Indian nation. When Prime Minister I.K. Gujral met Clinton, he was startled to find the American President's conversation peppered with references to Tharoor's book and stories of India's path to nationhood. (Gujral, who knew Tharoor personally, had not yet read the book.)

The success of the book and the attention it garnered, made Tharoor think about writing more non-fiction. By now, he had a real problem writing fiction. The reason: to create a world that a novel and its characters inhabit requires the author to keep an alternate reality in his or her mind. Even as Tharoor's responsibilities increased at the UN, he found it more and more difficult to keep this imaginary world intact in his head. He would return to the novel after, say, spending two weeks handling a crisis in Bosnia, and struggle to recapture the essence of his characters and the environment that he had created for them.

With non-fiction however, it was much easier. He would return to his manuscript, read some of what he had written, understand where the argument was going and pick up where he had left off. Once his UN career came to an end, Tharoor was finally free to write about the things he believed in.

We know what happened next. Tharoor took an extremely well-paid job in Dubai, made a million dollars or more, but longed to return to public service. The Congress party offered him a seat. But unlike most well-known people who are asked to join politics, he was not given the easy option of a Rajya Sabha seat. He would have to go to Thiruvananthapuram and fight a Lok Sabha election.

This was even harder than it seemed. Not only are Indian elections intensely complex and cut-throat affairs, but Tharoor had been a non-resident Malayali for most of his adult life. He had grown up in Mumbai, Kolkata and Delhi and had joined the UN right after university. He had very little idea of what things were like in Kerala.

As it turned out, the election campaign was tough— Tharoor brushed-up his Malayalam to make public speeches, but his candidacy was not helped by the attitude of the state Congress unit which believed that he was an outsider who had seized an opportunity.

Against the odds, Tharoor won and with the support of Sonia Gandhi and Manmohan Singh, became a minister right away. All went well. His erstwhile civil servant colleagues sang his praises. He was seen as the rising star of Indian politics.

And then, an unnecessary controversy erupted. Tharoor was accused of favouring a bid for a Kerala IPL team in which his girlfriend (later his wife) had a stake. As any IPL decision was not Tharoor's to make, it was hard to see how he had behaved improperly. But such was the media's feeding frenzy that he resigned. At the time, most people had assumed that he would pack his bags and go back abroad. Instead, to everyone's surprise, Shashi decided to stay on to fight his political battles.

One aspect of the resignation was that Tharoor had a lesser workload than he had as a minister. So he sat down with David Davidar and discussed whether he could go back to writing. Davidar was enthusiastic and Tharoor, who had never bothered about royalty rates before, realised that income from writing could help pay the bills. His MP salary was not enough to cover the office staff and travel required to nurse his constituency.

It is the books that Tharoor wrote during this phase, when he was out of office, that cemented his reputation as one of India's bestselling authors. Some of them seemed like natural follow-ups. He had already written a book for the sixtieth anniversary of Indian Independence in 2007 (*The Elephant, The Tiger, and the Cell Phone: Reflections on India, the Emerging 21st Century Power*), which had sold so well that his publishers were eagerly looking forward to his next.

Tharoor stayed loyal to Davidar, who had left Penguin, and went with him to Aleph which published Tharoor's biggest bestsellers. Some of them came about by sheer accident—for instance, Tharoor was invited to a literary festival at

Hay-on-Wye. The Oxford Union asked him to participate in a debate about colonialism (the exact subject was whether the UK should pay reparations to its former Colonies). It was a subject that Tharoor had strong views on so he agreed to take part.

His speech was good but even he was surprised by the overwhelming response when somebody posted it on YouTube, where it got two million views in a matter of days. Suddenly there was a renewed debate on the role of the British Raj. Even Tharoor-haters in the Right-wing loved it and when Prime Minister Modi spoke approvingly of the speech, there was no doubt that something unprecedented was going on.

David Davidar told Tharoor that he thought there was a book in the subject. Tharoor said no, there wasn't much more to be said. Everyone knew all this anyway. Davidar did not agree. No, the damaging consequences of the Empire on India had not been adequately discussed, he maintained. Otherwise, why would the video have had such an impact?

Finally, Tharoor agreed to do the book. But, he had a condition: it couldn't just cover the same ground as the speech. It had to be more substantial. So, for the first time in his writing career, Tharoor engaged researchers and made them look at specific aspects of British rule in India, such as the railways and the economy.

Then, he got lucky. The Bhutanese Ambassador called and asked if he would be free to meet the King who was going to be in Delhi. Tharoor said it would be his pleasure but he had no idea why the King would want to meet him. The Ambassador said he didn't know either but could he set up the meeting? Sure, said Tharoor.

When he did meet the King, Tharoor was surprised to discover that there was no political or formal agenda. The King had read Tharoor and simply wanted to meet an author he admired. Tharoor was flattered and delighted when the King invited him to Bhutan. He accepted the invitation but asked if he could be left undisturbed to write. Of course, said the King.

So Shashi Tharoor spent twelve days in Bhutan writing half of what eventually became *An Era of Darkness*. By the time he came back to Delhi, the entire book had taken shape in his mind and was easy to finish.

It proved to be his biggest bestseller yet—one of the biggest that India had seen in the hardback format. It still sells steadily and the British edition received enormous attention with Tharoor appearing on the BBC to discuss the evils of Empire.

Why did it do so well? Why is a new generation so fascinated by events that took place nearly a century ago?

Well, partly because it is an extraordinarily fluent and illuminating book. But its success is at least partly explained by the ignorance of a new generation that has forgotten what the freedom struggle was about.

That somebody who is so British in his manner should be so willing to clinically dissect the misdeeds of the British Raj surprised many young people. They did not realise that, in a sense, Tharoor was behaving exactly as Jawaharlal Nehru, and so many other British-educated liberals, had done in the run-up to Independence.

If *An Era of Darkness* had thrilled Right-wing elements who hated Tharoor otherwise, his next book succeeded in incensing them beyond all measure.

Tharoor had long been dismayed by the notion, assiduously spread by the sangh parivar, that those who did not subscribe to the RSS view of Hindutva were somehow anti-Hindu or even, not Hindu at all. He wanted to make it clear that there was a huge difference between Hinduism and Hindutva.

And that the RSS view of what Hinduism should be was a twentieth-century construct that had very little to do with Hindu philosophy which dated back centuries.

He wrote *Why I Am A Hindu*, its title deliberately echoing Bertrand Russell's *Why I Am Not a Christian* (not that the Hindutvawallas necessarily knew who Russell was) to demonstrate that Hinduism, with its open and liberal ethos, allowed even those of a not-particularly-ritualistic mindset to engage and keep faith.

Just as he had with the British Raj, he pulled no punches, taking on the RSS, the Hindu Mahasabha and all the other organisations that had tried to politicise Hinduism by adopting a narrow and restricted view.

The book was an instant bestseller. Like *An Era of Darkness*, it dominated debate and discourse for months after its publication. How Tharoor managed to sell a book that rubbished India's currently dominant ideology is a mystery to many and its success was taken (mistakenly, as it turned out) to suggest that perhaps Hindus were tiring of political Hindutva. And yet, despite the election results that returned the BJP to power, the book continues to sell steadily.

I asked Shashi Tharoor, when I met him for this book, what it was that made him happier. Did he like the idea that he was able to turn out bestseller after bestseller without dumbing down the issues he was discussing? Or (apart from the commercial success of the books) was he more pleased by the fact that his books influenced so many young people who had no idea (or the wrong ideas) about what Hinduism really said or what the Raj was about or what liberalism and secularism meant in the Indian context?

He did not hesitate in opting for the second. He loves writing. That much is clear. But, at least when it comes to non-fiction, he is not a man who writes because that is his calling. He writes only about the things that matter to him and if the books lead to a pan-Indian debate, then he is truly satisfied as an author.

Now that he is finally making money from his books, he is pleased to be a successful writer. But he is still the sort of guy to whom the reviews and the public impact matter much more than the sales.

After the Congress lost its second election in a row, Tharoor has to decide how involved he will be in politics for the next few years. Of course, he will continue to nurse his constituency. And of course he will remain an active parliamentarian.

But there are no ministries on the horizon and as the Congress passes through a transitional phase, trying to reinvent itself, there is probably a role for someone like Shashi Tharoor to play in the reconstruction of the party.

It is not clear to me whether he wants to pay such a role. During the last stint in Opposition, he did what the party expected of him, but never tried to get close to Rahul Gandhi or to ask for organisational power and responsibilities. Perhaps he will maintain that same balance in the future, despite Sonia Gandhi taking over as interim president of the party.

Meanwhile, he still has to fight off a criminal charge for abetment to suicide, emerging from the death of his wife in a Delhi hotel. Though the case was originally about murder, the police found no evidence that she was killed. They have now decided she committed suicide and charged Shashi Tharoor with abetment. Obviously, he regards the whole thing as a political vendetta but equally there is no doubt that it will take up much of his time.

But my guess is he will keep writing. He still has things to say. And there are readers who are willing to pay to read them.